Process Problem Solving

A Guide for Maintenance and Operations Teams

Process Problem Solving

A Guide for Maintenance and Operations Teams

By Bob Sproull

Productivity Press
PORTLAND, OREGON

Additional copies of this book and a learning package for leading a book study group are available from the publisher. Discounts are available for multiple copies through the Sales Department (800-394-6868). Address all other inquiries to:

Productivity Press
P.O. Box 13390
Portland OR 97213-0390
United States of America
Telephone: 503-235-0600
Fax: 503-235-0909
E-mail: info@productivityinc.com

Cover designed by Stephen Scates
Page design and composition by William H. Brunson, Typography Services
Printed and bound by Malloy in the United States of America

Library of Congress Cataloging-in-Publication Data

Sproull, Robert
    The problem-solving handbook / Robert Sproull.
        p.   cm.
    ISBN 1-56327244-X
    1. Plant maintenance—Handbooks, manuals, etc.   2. Problem-solving
Handbooks, manuals, etc.   I. Title.

TS192.S68   2001
658.4'03—dc21   00–069931

05 04 03 02 01   5 4 3 2 1

Dedication

For all of the gifts they have given me, I dedicate this book to the following individuals. To my best friend—my wife, Beverly, for her enduring belief in me and years of patience, support, advice, and love. To my son, Robbie, for teaching me to contemplate my thoughts before sharing them; and my other son, John, for teaching me the edifying lesson of never being satisfied with what I've done. To my daughter, Emily, for teaching me the value of a smile and a positive attitude toward life. And to my second best friend, Bob Ostendorf, for mentoring me and giving me the opportunity to learn, grow, and experience all that turnarounds have to offer.

Bob Sproull

Contents

Preface

Problems, problems, problems—everyone seems to have problems. Every process or system, no matter what it may be, eventually will become unacceptable to someone in some way; that is, it will develop a problem. The speed and efficacy with which the problem is solved depends, to a large degree, on the skills of the people assigned to fix it—on how well they systematically investigate, study, and analyze the problem for its root cause. Herein lies a dilemma for many organizations: their people often do not possess problem-solving skills. For example, people commonly treat the *symptoms* of a problem rather than addressing its root cause. When this happens, the problem never really is eradicated; it simply becomes latent.

Such misdirection is especially evident in typical manufacturing maintenance troubleshooting efforts, with the net effect being extended periods of equipment downtime. It isn't because maintenance employees aren't intelligent, and it isn't because they don't care; it's because many companies fail to provide adequate training for this select group. However, there is reason for hope: problem solving is a demonstrable skill that can be learned and applied, and *Process Problem Solving* was developed to show you how.

Although *Process Problem Solving* was created to meet the needs of plant maintenance troubleshooters, it is versatile enough to be adapted to any other discipline. The book is simple, in that the techniques described are easy to learn and use, yet it is also comprehensive in its approach to solving problems. Although many of the examples included in *Process*

Problem Solving are equipment related, I have added other nonequipment problems to emphasize the versatility of the tools presented.

Numerous theories exist regarding the best method for learning, and I have tried to incorporate as many of these as possible into the framework of this book. One important principle of adult learning is to "learn, then apply": as you learn new techniques, you must apply them immediately to real-world situations. If you want to develop a great golf swing, for example, it is imperative that you continue to learn new techniques and then apply them. We all know, though, that to do so correctly requires practice, practice, and practice! Another theory suggests that you should introduce information "one layer at a time," rather than all at once. Still other theories tell us that learning is achieved by "doing."

Thus, I have included a variety of learning aids in *Process Problem Solving*. At the beginning of each chapter, a box entitled "What You Should Learn in This Chapter" alerts you in advance to important lessons contained within the chapter. To complement this, a "key words" box at the beginning of each individual section of each chapter advises you of specific topics of interest within that section. These boxed entries emphasize the importance of major concepts, techniques, and tools as you encounter them in the text.

Rather than include a chapter summary of important principles that you should have learned, at the end of each chapter I have added a lined box, "What did you learn?," where you can record your knowledge. I also prompt you to compare your notes to "What You Should Learn in This Chapter" (located at the beginning of each chapter). If any major discrepancies between the content in the two boxes occur, you should review the chapter for material that you may not have grasped.

Throughout the book, I use real-world examples that should resonate with your own past experiences. At the end of each chapter, a "Problem Assignment" prompts you to practice the use of various tools and techniques. This is an important step in learning, so please do complete these assignments.

You also will find many "Problem-Solving Truths"—axioms and clichés that are woven into the text and intended to reinforce important concepts, be thought provoking, and serve as learning aids that emphasize key lessons.

Finally, in the Appendix, I have included a collection of problem-solving case studies that primarily utilize the problem analysis flow (PAF) chart and other tools for resolution. These case studies cover a variety of subjects and problems and will appeal to a wide array of readers. Some case studies include a completed PAF chart that allows you to practice what you've learned. As you move through the individual case studies, fill in each section of the PAF chart without consulting the completed one. When you complete your PAF chart, compare it to the completed version. Again, if yours and mine differ, investigate why.

It is very important that you read Chapter 1, "Understanding Problems," first. It provides a comprehensive look at what a problem is and why it is so important to use a structured approach, and it also identifies potential problem-solving traps that predictably yet stealthily frustrate problem solvers. Chapter 2, "Selecting the Right Problem," introduces quantitative methods for prioritizing and ultimately selecting the problems whose resolution results in the biggest payback. In Chapter 3, "Problem-Solving Teams," I present some helpful suggestions, based on my own experiences, on the make-up of the team and offer a brief look at simple team dynamics. Many excellent books on team dynamics are available, so I cover this subject superficially only, presenting what I feel are important lessons for problem-solving teams.

In Chapter 4, "The Why-Why? Tools in Problem Solving," I introduce and examine some of the fundamental and essential tools needed to solve problems, along with relevant examples of how each one is used. The question "Why?" is the cornerstone of all these tools. In Chapter 5, "The Inquisition Tools," additional, supplementary problem-solving tools are presented, once again with examples. These tools, as the chapter title implies, are used to answer What?, When?, How?, and so on. In Chapter 6, "The Problem Analysis Flow (PAF) Chart," I present what I believe is one of the most powerful tools you will ever use. The PAF chart incorporates many of the basic tools described in Chapters 4 and 5 into a single tool that will ultimately direct you to a problem's root cause.

I sincerely hope that this book will provide you with an enriching, positive learning experience and will help you become more successful at recognizing and solving problems. Solving problems should be a rewarding experience, and I believe that if you utilize *Process Problem Solving* in the manner I have intended, your proficiency for solving problems will increase significantly. Good luck!

Bob Sproull

Bob Sproull provides both consulting services
and on-site Problem-Solving Workshops.
For further information, contact:

BOB SPROULL
401 Country Lane
Morgantown, PA 19543
610-913-0933 or
toll free: 866-913-0933

Acknowledgments

This book would not have been possible without the contributions of several important people. First of all, I would like to recognize Don Makie, a friend and fellow consultant, for recognizing the value of the message I had to give and for encouraging me to have my work published. Thanks, Don.

Also, I would like to thank my editors, Michael Ryder and Robert Saigh, for their gift of turning my manuscript into a professional text. Without them, the book in its present form would not exist. Thanks, Michael and Robert.

Bill Brunson, of William H. Brunson Typography Services, designed and composed the book with skill and efficiency; and Stephen Scates of Productivity brought the same attributes to his cover design. Thank you, gentlemen.

Bob Sproull

CHAPTER 1

Understanding Problems

What You Should Learn in This Chapter

Why problems are considered problems.
Why a structured approach to problem solving is
necessary. The logical pathway to problem solving.
The kind of things that get in your way when
trying to solve problems.

One reason people have difficulty solving a problem is that they truly don't understand the nature of the problem. When someone commands, "Fix that problem now!," there's probably no connection between the problem that needs fixing and the person charged with fixing it. That is, there is no ownership of the problem.

Understanding why a problem is considered as such is one of the first steps in solving it. Furthermore, this understanding helps to create an appropriate sense of urgency for both the organization and its problem solvers.

In this first section of the book, we will develop a complete definition of problems and dissect them to better understand their framework and structure. In addition to defining problems we will discuss a variety of related subjects, including:

- The necessity of a structured approach to problem solving
- The logical pathway to problem solving
- The need to draw upon basic reasoning, common sense, and imagination

1

- Potential problem-solving traps that get in the way of problem solvers
- Specific types of problems and how they should be addressed
- Important documentation

As in all chapters, we will finish with a problem assignment to practice what we have learned.

1.1 WHAT IS A PROBLEM?

What Is a Problem?

Performance
Negative Deviation
Cause Unknown
Solution Unknown

Webster defines a problem in simple terms as "a matter proposed for solution: a puzzle." Although this simple definition describes what a problem is from a literal perspective, it hardly provides enough insight to understand what a problem really is in the real world.

Kepner and Tregoe[1] define problems as deviations from expected performance. They have developed a simple model to illustrate the structure of a problem, as shown in Figure 1-1.

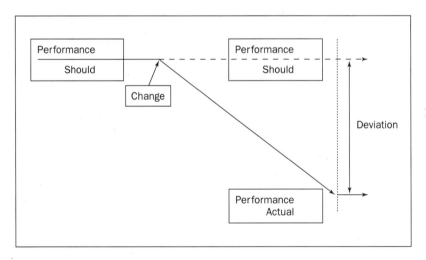

Figure 1-1.

Kepner and Tregoe explain that "a performance standard is achieved when all conditions required for acceptable performance are operating as they should." This is true for everything in the work environment, including people, systems, equipment, departments, and so on. Their model tells us that a level of performance should be occurring; then, a change takes place, and a new level of performance is observed. The difference between the old level of performance and the new level of performance is a deviation. Is this deviation referred to as a problem? Let us answer that question.

In my experience, a problem is not merely a deviation from the expected level of performance. As a matter of fact, in order for a deviation to be classified as a problem I believe it must satisfy one or more of the following three basic requirements:

1. The deviation must be perceived as being negative to the organization. That is, the deviation must result in a loss of production, quality, safety, etc., that translates into a delivery shortfall, a loss in revenue, customer dissatisfaction, a throughput issue, an injury, etc.
2. The cause of the deviation is unknown. That is, the root cause is not immediately established using the "normal" problem-solving techniques, thus causing the change in performance to linger. Obviously, if the cause isn't known, then the solution cannot be known either.
3. The root cause and the solution are both known, but the solution can't be implemented because doing so would either cost too much or take too long. As pressure mounts to have the problem fixed, the symptoms get treated or another "quick fix" is found that, in turn, creates a prolonged episode of the problem.

If the root cause and the solution are known, and implementing the solution doesn't take too long and/or cost too much, then the deviation is not considered a problem because it just gets fixed! In short, deviations in and of themselves may or may not become problems. When you add in the critical factors of cost, time, and lost revenues, however, deviations most likely will become problems. What if an organization considers a deviation to be positive? Say the change that occurs results in better safety, quality, production, or revenue. Is it still considered a problem? What happens if this deviation results in an improvement to safety, quality, or increased throughput that can't be explained in terms of the origin of this deviation (i.e., no root cause)? Is this or could this be a problem? The answer is a resounding yes! When a positive deviation returns to its *previously acceptable level of performance* (and it will if we don't address the root cause), the organization will now perceive the deviation as being negative and, therefore, it will become a problem (see Figure 1-2). For this reason, it is imperative that *all* deviations be investigated for root cause with the same level

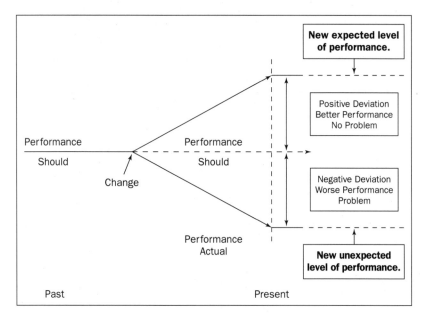

Figure 1-2.

of intensity. In other words, all changes in performance (deviations) have the potential to become problems.

Problem-Solving Truth #1: *All problems are the direct result of changes that occurred prior to the new level of performance.*

Problem-Solving Truth #2: *Deviations in performance don't become problems unless they negatively have an impact on the organization, their root cause is unknown, or it costs too much or takes too much time to fix them.*

1.2 PROBLEM-SOLVING SKILLS

As a general rule, I believe most people become excited and exhilarated when they solve a problem. There is actually a physiological reason that explains these emotions. When people get excited—when they do something that they feel good about, such

> **Problem Solving**
> Skills
> Failures & Success
> Positive Rewards
> Security

as solving a problem—the brain emits endorphins. Endorphins are the purest opiate in the world. So, people in a sense truly do get "high" when they solve a problem. Their level of satisfaction actually seems to be proportional to the size and complexity of the problem and to how severe the problem is perceived by the organization.

But if people feel so good when they solve problems, why is it so many individuals look for ways to avoid them? Kepner and Tregoe tell us that the answer depends on the presence of one or more of the following four conditions:

1. People don't have the skills needed to solve problems.
2. People haven't experienced success in solving problems.

3. People have never been positively reinforced when they successfully solved problems.
4. People are afraid to fail.

People actively will avoid problem-solving opportunities if they lack the proper skills, haven't successfully solved problems in the past, aren't appreciated when they do solve problems, or feel threatened by the situation. Let's explore these conditions in a bit more detail.

Why is it that some people lack the skills needed to solve problems? They do their jobs flawlessly every day, but give them a problem to solve and they're lost. Are they stupid? Do they just not get it? Based upon my experience, the answer lies in the level of training (if any) they have received. The American educational system certainly doesn't prepare one to solve problems! There is a difference between being educated and having common sense or being logical. Some people are blessed with an inordinate amount of common sense and logic; others are not. The latter group must be trained in problem solving.

However, many organizations do not understand the importance of training and learning. Two participants in one of my workshops had worked for their company for 27 years and had never received any training on problem solving. This is a sad state of affairs. I believe that many people who think they haven't experienced success at problem solving actually have, but they don't realize it because they have never been positively rewarded. At one time or another, everyone has solved a problem!

Kepner and Tregoe also tell us that some people are afraid to fail, so they shy away from attempting to solve problems. Why are they afraid to fail? Consider children in Little League baseball, whose frantic parents berate them for striking out or making an error. Similar behavior occurs in the workplace. Sometimes, even when problems are solved, negative feedback occurs with statements such as, "What took you so long?" Such comments are unlikely to stimulate people to go forth and look for new problems to solve! People must be made to feel good about themselves when they solve a problem, and they must be allowed to fail or they will stop trying! In the process of learning, mistakes will be made. As long as we learn from those mistakes and aren't criticized for them, we will move in a positive direction and continue learning.

Problem solving is a skill that can be learned, and success can be achieved when this skill is utilized. In order for this to occur, however, the right management environment must exist, one that supports a structured approach to problem solving and rewards and recognizes successes. When people solve problems, they must be praised. When they fail, they must be made to feel secure enough to try again. As their skills are applied to new areas and their expertise improves, failures will be replaced by successes.

I've heard many managers say that structured problem-solving methods take too long to implement. They demand immediate action. Yet, systematic methods only *appear* to take longer than the typical "change something and see what happens" approach. In the end, the results of the former are *solved* problems, rather than symptoms that have been temporarily treated but inevitably will reappear. Management, which I believe is the root of many problems (actually, I believe management is involved in 95 percent of all problems), must be patient and supportive; it is truly worth the wait and the effort.

Problem-Solving Truth #3: *People will avoid problem-solving opportunities if they lack problem-solving skills, haven't successfully solved problems in the past, aren't appreciated when they do solve problems, or feel threatened by the situation.*

Problem-Solving Truth #4: *Systematic methods only appear to take longer than the "change something and see what happens" approach.*

1.3 THE NEED FOR A STRUCTURED APPROACH

Problem solving need not be a difficult, time-consuming ordeal, but that is exactly how many people perceive it. Usually, these same people try something—anything—just to see what happens, and then repeat the process until they either get frustrated

Structured Approach
L. U. C. K.
Root Cause
Hunches/Intuition
Expected

and quit or luck onto the root cause. I have always believed that luck plays a major role in solving a problem, but the luck I'm referring to is **L**aboring **U**nder **C**orrect **K**nowledge, or L.U.C.K.! This represents a structured approach.

Everyone at one time or another has witnessed a problem that was allegedly solved, only to reappear. When this happens, it generally means that rather than having found the true root cause of the problem, we simply treated one or more of its symptoms. The reason most problems aren't truly fixed is because the "fixer" doesn't follow a systematic or structured approach to get to the root cause of the problem. Mechanics or servicepeople typically investigate a problem until they find something wrong and then assume that what they find is the source of the problem. In reality, they probably found a symptom, "band-aided" it, and then quit. The auto mechanic who fixes your stalling car and the air conditioner serviceperson who fixes your heat pump cut-off problem are two everyday examples.

There are many advantages to using a structured approach in problem solving. In fact, a structured approach will:

1. Reduce the probability that key factors contributing to the problem will be overlooked.

2. Force us to re-evaluate and understand the basic process with the problem.
3. Discourage reliance on hunches, intuition, and the "I know what the problem is" syndrome.
5. Increase the probability that the root cause or causes of the problem will be found.
6. Result in solved problems.

Contrary to popular belief, problem-solving success does not result from superior knowledge. Certainly, it helps to understand the process as well as the problem, but total knowledge of the object experiencing the problem is not a prerequisite for solving the problem. What is important is being able to use problem-solving tools effectively.

When organizational pressures to fix a problem quickly become too great, many people panic and simply attempt to "fix" it without finding out what caused it. Replacing a fuse instead of finding out why the fuse blew in the first place and using a jumper to bypass a circuit instead of locating the cause of the short are two examples of "fixing" a problem without knowing what caused it. As we already have stated, if we don't know what caused a problem, the problem will return.

A structured approach to problem solving will succeed only if such an approach is established as the norm. A shift in problem-solving expectations is just as important as teaching and learning new skills. Failure to set expectations—that is, failure to demand that the root cause of problems be uncovered—will seriously impede any effort to upgrade problem solving in any organization. For example, in one company I conducted five workshops on problem solving. The general manager was concerned that he hadn't seen a shift in success at solving problems. I attended one of his daily production meetings and listened as everyone presented a seemingly endless list of problems to solve; never once was the question of root causes raised. However, when the GM began expecting root cause analysis, the shift to solved problems was immediate and swift!

Problem-Solving Truth #5: Problem-solving success is not the result of superior knowledge.

Problem-Solving Truth #6: Structured approaches to solving problems will only be successful if they are established as the norm.

Problem-Solving Truth #7: Today's problem solutions could very well be tomorrow's problems if the right questions aren't asked.

Problem-Solving Truth #8: Generally speaking, today's problems are yesterday's solutions implemented without data.

1.4 THE LOGICAL PATHWAY OF PROBLEM SOLVING

Now that we can see the advantages of using a structured, systematic problem-solving approach, one that is founded upon basic reasoning and logic, let's look at a typical problem-solving format. Many problem-solving formats exist, but all use, in some form or another, the following elements of a logical pathway:

Logical Pathway

Identify
Describe & Define
List Symptoms
List Changes
Analyze
Hypothesize
Test Causes
Take Action
Test/Implement Solution
Implement Controls

1. Identify the problem.
2. Describe and define the problem.
3. List the symptoms.
4. List the known changes.
5. Analyze the problem.

6. Hypothesize possible causes.
7. Test possible causes.
8. Take action(s) on the cause(s).
9. Test and implement the solution.
10. Implement appropriate controls.

Let's explore each of these in a bit more detail.

Identify the Problem

Earlier, we defined a problem as a deviation from an expected level of performance, without a known cause or solution, which negatively has an impact on an organization. In order to identify and ultimately solve a problem effectively, we must know exactly what the expected level of performance should be compared to what the actual performance is now. We must also understand the effect of the deviation on the organization and why it is considered negative (or positive).

Describe and Define the Problem

Effectively describing and defining the problem is, in some respects, the most important step in the problem-solving process. The problem description builds the foundation for the problem-solving activities that follow, so it must be as complete and accurate as possible. For example, suppose you were given the task of solving a problem involving a motor that stopped functioning. Because you had solved a similar problem in the past, you assumed that the root cause was a burned-out armature. By limiting yourself only to actions that might be related to things like a defective overload or a short in the electrical system, you may miss other potential causes of the problem. What if the real root cause was seized bearings that resulted in excessive heat build up, which in turn shut the motor down?

When describing the problem, it helps to view it from two separate perspectives: the object and the object's defect or fault.

By asking a series of simple questions, it is possible to develop a more complete definition of the problem, as follows:

a. *What* is the specific object with the problem and what feature of the object is considered to have a fault or defect? In other words, what is it and what's wrong with it?
b. *Where* geographically and physically on the object is the problem or fault found?
c. *When* in time and when in the process cycle of the object was the problem first observed?
d. *How many* objects have the problem, and how many faults or defects are observed on the objects?
e. *What* is the trend and scope of the defect or fault? Is the problem rate increasing, decreasing, or remaining constant? Is there a distinct pattern for the defect or fault?

It is helpful to answer these questions by contrasting or comparing the object with the problem to another like it (or to a similar object) without the problem. That is, ask not only where the problem is, but also where it is not. Or, where would you expect to see the problem but you do not? These comparisons help you zero in on distinctions that are important to consider in your effort to solve the problem. When this step is complete, you should combine all that you know about the problem and then develop a *problem statement*.

List the Symptoms

Solving problems is the culmination of many different activities, one of the most important of which is developing a list of symptoms related to the problem. If you have ever been a patient in an emergency room at a hospital, then perhaps you have observed the actions of the ER doctors and nurses.

Doctors understand that developing a list of symptoms is paramount to a precise diagnosis of their patients. What information interests doctors? They, or their nurses, usually check your temperature, your blood pressure, your pulse rate, your eyes, your ears, your abdomen for painful areas, your lungs, and so on. Doctors are clearly searching your body for symptoms that might lead them to the root cause of your ailment.

Doctors use hearing, sight, touch, and smell to detect outward and inward signs of a malady, and you, too, must use your senses and search for symptoms that will lead you to the root cause of the problem you are investigating.

If you're in a typical manufacturing setting, you might detect common symptoms through smell, touch, sound, or vision. Although you must use all of your senses when searching for symptoms, you will, in fact, identify more symptoms by sight than by all your other senses.

Below are listed some real-world examples of symptoms that you will find as your problem-solving effort progresses.

Smell
- If you smell the odor of burning rubber, you might look for worn or loose V-belts or an electrical problem or a problem with overheating bearings.
- If you smell the odor of burning plastic (or rubber depending upon the type of insulation), you might look for an electrical problem like a short in a motor, electrical cords, overheating coils, defective junction boxes, etc.

Touch
- If you feel abnormal vibration, you might look for worn bearings in a motor, loose-fitting bolts on a motor, misalignment of shafts, etc.

13

- If you feel abnormal temperatures, you might look for worn bearings, blocked ventilation or coolant lines, inoperative coolant pumps, electrical problems, etc.

Sound
- If you hear a grinding or scraping noise, you might look for misalignments or actual misaligned gears, shafts, or pistons.
- If you hear a rattling noise, you might look for loose or missing fittings or screws, an excessive gap or play between two mating parts, etc.

Vision
- You can detect many things by sight:
  - Fluid levels or leaks
  - Abnormal functioning of equipment
  - Changes in color or consistency
  - Excessive gaps
  - Slippage
  - Jerking motions
  - Fluctuating gages
  - Cracking or burring

List the Known Changes

Earlier, I said that problems are the direct result of changes that have occurred prior to the new level of performance. The change or changes responsible for the new level of perform-ance could have occurred immediately prior to the problem or in the distant past. For this reason, *all* known changes must be listed and investigated.

In many organizations this is a problem because changes are made frequently but are not documented. In this case, you may be forced to reconstruct changes based upon interviews with process owners. It is vitally important to document any change made to the process, including changes in raw material lots, actions taken to repair or improve processes, changes in equipment settings, and the like. This is so crucial that I cannot over-emphasize it! If your company does not document changes exhaustively, then you must force this improvement!

Analyze the Problem

Once you have developed a complete, accurate description of the problem, and have listed all changes and symptoms, you must now begin an analysis of the problem based upon this information. Effective problem analysis attempts to relate the problem to symptoms, differences, changes, and times. In other words, you wish to determine what is different or distinctive between what the problem is and what it is not, where the problem is or is not, or when the problem occurs or does not.

Once you have determined the differences, you search for changes relative to the differences. Once you have identified changes relative to the differences, you must then determine when these changes occurred. Once you have collected these four puzzle pieces—symptoms, differences, changes, and times— you are ready to form hypotheses for possible causes. It is important to understand that problems might have multiple root causes!

Hypothesize Possible Causes

Once you've completed your analysis of the problem (i.e. symptoms, differences, changes, and times), you can create a list of potential causes. This is not a guess list, but rather the result of a logical, systematic look at the information you have been able to collect to this point. Carefully answer the question, "Based upon the information I have gathered, how could this change have caused this problem at this time?" Because the list of possible causes is logically developed, it reduces the likelihood of and reliance on hunches and intuition. If you need more data or information to develop this list thoroughly and make it more usable, then collect what you need. Effective possible cause lists are a combination of experience, good data, and the expertise of you and your co-workers. And don't be afraid to ask for help if you need it; it's a sign of intelligence!

Test Possible Causes

A list of possible causes constructed according to a logical and factual approach should contain realistic potential causes. The next step is to distill this list into a shorter list of most probable causes by testing each possible cause against a pre-determined set of test criteria. Using something as simple as an "if-then" statement, one can develop these test criteria quite simply. Use a simple question such as, "If I increase the voltage, then (some event) should happen." Each possible cause must be looked at individually and only the survivors will be considered as the most probable causes. The final list must then be tested in more depth to further zero in on the final root cause (or causes). *Don't ever assume* a problem has only one cause.

Take Action(s) on the Cause(s)

Once the list of potential causes has been refined to a manageable level, you must decide upon the most appropriate action(s), if any, to take. Several actions or combinations of actions are possible:

1. Take no action and decide to live with the problem.
2. Take a short-term action that effectively will buy you some time.
3. Take a long-term corrective action that eliminates the problem.

Usually, we opt for a combination of 2 and 3. The priority is to stop the negative effect of the problem first and then to implement true preventive actions. Whatever the action taken, we should always consider its potential impact on the process and the controls that can be put in place to prevent a recurrence of the problem. An example of this is adding a check as part of the preventive maintenance on the equipment.

Test and Implement the Solution

Repeatedly, I have seen problem-solving teams go through a complete analysis of a problem, develop solutions, implement them, and then assume that they have fixed the problem. *Never* implement a solution without validating that your solution does not have a negative impact on the process in question! Always perform a first-piece inspection (and possibly a more extensive inspection) to assure that the product being produced meets all performance requirements.

I am reminded of a problem-solving team at a large sheet molding compound (SMC) supplier that was absolutely certain that its root cause analysis had led it to the problem-solving "Promised Land." The team had done an excellent job of determining why a bonding machine always seemed to bond components out of position. This team was so confident that they had implemented the solution and left the premises to celebrate. After all, this had been one of the plant's single biggest problems, and the team had done what no others had been able to do! While celebrating though, the equipment produced thirty-five scrap parts. The "improvement" had actually altered the position of another component, and the team had failed to test production after making the change! Remember: today's solutions could very well be tomorrow's problems. And again, always test the impact of your solution before you declare success!

Implement Appropriate Controls

Once the root cause has been identified and a solution tested and implemented, it is extremely important that you also implement controls to prevent the problem from recurring. These controls might be, for instance, an update to the preventive maintenance (PM) checklist or a control chart of the measurable associated with the problem. The critical point is that you never walk away from a solved problem without implementing preventive measures and/or controls.

Problem-Solving Truth #9: When describing a problem, always view the problem from two separate perspectives: the object and the object's defect or fault.

Problem-Solving Truth #10: Use all of your senses when searching for symptoms.

Problem-Solving Truth #11: Effective problem analysis attempts to relate the problem to symptoms, differences, changes, and times.

Problem-Solving Truth #12: It is important to understand that problems might have multiple root causes.

Problem-Solving Truth #13: Identifying potential problem causes is the result of a logical and systematic look at all available information. It is never the result of guessing.

Problem-Solving Truth #14: Don't ever be afraid to ask for help when solving problems. Asking for help is not a weakness; it is a sign of intelligence.

Problem-Solving Truth #15: Don't ever assume a problem has only one cause.

Problem-Solving Truth #16: The priority in problem solving is always stopping the negative effect of the problem first, then implementing true solutions and preventive actions.

Problem-Solving Truth #17: *Never implement a solution and then assume it is failsafe. Always validate that your solution does not have a negative impact on the process in question. Always test the impact of your solution before you declare success.*

1.5 REASON, GOOD JUDGEMENT, AND COMMON SENSE

The best problem-solving tools in the world are of little value if we ignore reason, good judgement, and common sense. No tool ever should completely replace these attributes. With that in mind, here are eight important problem-solving fundamentals one must consider:

Common Sense
Accurate Definitions
Simultaneous Symptoms
Independent Causes
DFCs
Distinctions
Changes

1. *Develop a complete definition of the problem.* If this is not the most important fundamental, it certainly is close to it. It is absolutely imperative that you totally understand the problem before attempting to solve it.

   I am reminded of a problem-solving effort involving a motor attached to a robotic arm that was used to cut fiberglass parts. This particular motor had burned up five times and had been replaced five times. I was asked to get involved and assist with the resolution of the problem. My first question to the team that had been working on the problem was, "What do you mean when you say the motor burned up?" The team told me the armature was shorting out. My second question was, "What did you see when you opened the motor casing?" The team's response was to stare at me like deer in the headlights. It seems that no one

19

had actually looked inside the casing to further define the problem. They had assumed that it was an electrical failure. When we opened the motor, we found burned-out bearings. The team redefined the problem accordingly and was able to determine that a flow switch used to regulate coolant was mislocated and that the motor bearings were not being cooled correctly.

It bears repeating: you must make sure that you thoroughly understand the problem at hand and use every means available to define it completely.

2. *Develop accurate definitions of symptoms.* Symptoms are a sign that something has changed or gone wrong. They are the faults that we see, hear, smell, and feel (or taste, if you are a chef or cook). A machine that begins to make a funny noise; the smell of burning rubber or plastic; the feel of a vibration; a change in the appearance of a product characteristic—all are symptoms of a potential problem. Use all your senses to find all the symptoms.

3. *Look for simultaneous symptoms.* They usually have a common cause. When two or more symptoms occur at the same time, they typically have a common cause or origin, even if one is the result of the other. For example, two presses powered by the same compressed air source both fail at the same time.

4. *Independent causes may or may not occur simultaneously.* When symptoms are not simultaneous in occurrence, then they most likely are the result of independent problems and causes.

5. *Find defect-free configurations (DFCs).* They could lead you to the true root cause(s). Configurations are individual parts linked together to perform a given function. A defect-free configuration is the

combination of components in a nonfunctioning system, machine, or process that is still functioning correctly. DFCs could also include another identical or similar process or piece of equipment.

6. *Look for distinctions.* When comparing a nonfunctioning piece of equipment to another that is functioning (or to a similar piece of functioning equipment), what is unique, different, or special about it?

7. *List and investigate changes.* A change is any event that precedes the initial onset of a symptom of a problem. Because the change precedes the problem, it is a potential cause of the problem. It is important to remember that changes do not always occur immediately prior to the onset of the problem. The change may have happened long before the first symptom appeared, and the first symptom may have appeared long before you noticed it.

8. *Always test to determine cause(s).* Never solely rely on what you think is happening!

When attempting to solve a problem, make sure that common sense prevails and let your imagination and creative juices flow!

Problem-Solving Truth #18: *Never let any problem-solving tool completely replace your ability to reason and exercise good judgment.*

Problem-Solving Truth #19: *Symptoms are always a sign that something has changed or gone wrong.*

Problem-Solving Truth #20: *Simultaneous symptoms usually have a common cause.*

Problem-Solving Truth #21: *Independent causes may or may not occur simultaneously.*

Problem-Solving Truth #22: *Find defect-free configurations and then compare to find differences and distinctions.*

1.6 POTENTIAL PROBLEM-SOLVING TRAPS

Solving a problem, like any other activity, is not always as straightforward as some tools and techniques would lead you to believe. In the real world, there always seems to be obstacles that get in the way and/or lead the problem solver on a wild goose chase. Although you can't eliminate

Potential Traps

Erroneous Information
Defective Parts
Defective Gages
Defective Raw Material
Incorrect Drawings
Incorrect Logic

these traps, it is important that you are aware that they exist. Being on guard against them will help you stay on the path to the root cause of the problem. Typical traps that you should be aware of include the following.

- *Erroneous information, facts, or data supplied by someone involved in the process with the problem.* This misinformation could be supplied deliberately in an attempt to sabotage the process for personal gain (for instance, to attain time off due to equipment downtime), or unintentionally by someone just trying to be helpful who doesn't understand the importance of accurate information. Be wary of generalized statements such as, "It's always been like this," "I think it happened last week," or any statements that are based on emotion. When in doubt, collect new data or seek new information from other sources.
- *Defective replacement parts from the supplier.* Being trusting people, we automatically assume that if we take a replacement part out of the box, it must be functional.

Believe it or not, this is not always the case! If you are reasonably certain that one of the equipment parts is defective, and you install a replacement part and it doesn't correct the problem, my advice to you is to remove the replacement part and have it tested for functionality, just to be sure.

- *Defective measurement tools or gauges.* I am reminded of a team working on a rather large hydraulic press with a hot oil problem. The team had tried everything they could think of to solve the problem, but they could not locate its root cause. The team had made one fatal mistake in analyzing the problem: they had assumed that all of the gages on the press were functioning properly and, in particular, that the pressure readings were accurate (one of the known causes for hot oil is excessive pressure). When I explained the concept of problem-solving traps to them, the team checked all gages and found that the pressure gage was not giving accurate information. The actual delivered pressure was much higher than the gage reading. The team replaced the defective gage, adjusted the pressure into the normal operating range, and thus solved the problem. Incorrect data are actually more dangerous than no data, because it leads you down the wrong path.

- *Defective input material.* Raw material accepted as being good that is actually out-of-spec can create a trap. Raw material characteristics that affect the final product can lead you to the wrong conclusions. For example, one of the most important characteristics of sheet molding compound (SMC) is viscosity. If the viscosity moves outside the acceptable range, the material will exhibit different flow properties inside the mold. One team I worked with was trying to solve a surface quality problem. Because the tag on the batch of SMC had an acceptable value for viscosity, the team assumed that viscosity was not the root cause. When they retested the material, however, they found the viscosity to be too high, thus creating a material flow problem. This was the root cause of the problem. If one assumes that the material characteristic (i.e., viscosity) is acceptable when it isn't, wrong assumptions and conclusions will be the end product. When in doubt, retest!

- *Incorrect drawings or schematics.* How often in your company have modifications been made to equipment without the related drawings or schematics being updated? Even subtle changes to the process wiring, hydraulics, or such must be added to the drawings in a timely manner. When this fails to occur, drawings and schematics become a trap for future problem solvers.

  One team, which worked on a programmable, robotic cutting machine used to cut holes in fiberglass parts, made an important discovery regarding the placement of a limit switch that controlled the supply of coolant to the cutting motor. In so doing they corrected a problem that had been a source of significant downtime and quality losses and had diligently "marked up" the drawing to show the previous and new locations for the limit switch. The only problem was, they didn't file the drawing or share the findings with maintenance millwrights and electricians on the back shifts. When the same problem occurred on an identical cutting machine, the back-shift millwrights and electricians, without the benefit of the team's findings, simply replaced the flow switch in its old location, and the problem recurred.

  Communicate updates both verbally and in drawings and schematics so that everyone can benefit from them.

- *Incorrect logic on your part.* Even though you have thoroughly thought through a problem, it's possible that your assumptions may be erroneous or inaccurate. Therefore, it is always good practice to have someone else review your conclusions. Far from being a sign of weakness, doing so actually shows foresight.

These are some of the traps ready to spring up and lure you down the wrong problem-solving pathway. Beware of them!

Problem-Solving Truth #23: *Problem-solving traps create detours for problem solvers. You can't eliminate them, but it helps to know they exist.*

Problem-Solving Truth #24: *Incorrect data are actually more dangerous than no data because they lead you down the wrong path.*

1.7 INTERMITTENT AND RECURRING PROBLEMS

Intermittent Problems

Have you ever worked on a problem where symptoms appear, then disappear, then reappear, and so on? This is referred to as an intermittent problem, and it can be frustrating and sometimes difficult both to recognize and to solve. Once again, however, if you follow a systematic

Problems
Intermittent
Recurring
Disappearing Symptoms
Timing of Events
Periodic, Cyclic, Random
No Root Cause

approach, you will significantly reduce the degree of difficulty. One of the keys to solving this type problem is to spend lots of time on the process in question.

To find the root cause of intermittent problem, you must determine the timing of the symptoms. A simple yet effective procedure to do so follows.

1. Document each time the symptom(s) appear and disappear. It is important to record specific dates and times, including when the symptom(s) began and ended (duration).

   Document all changes that occur prior to and immediately after the onset of the symptoms. Operator shifts, environmental conditions (e.g., temperatures before and after, humidity before and after), operating speeds, material changes, and the like are all potentially useful clues that may help solve the problem.

2. Using a program like Excel, or even graph paper, create a simple time-based run chart (see Section 5.2 for details and a relevant example) depicting start and stop times for each occurrence of the symptom(s).

3. Transpose the documented changes directly onto the graph at the appropriate date and time coordinates.

4. Look for a correlation between the documented changes and the date/time that the symptoms occurred.

5. Analyze the plotted results. Is there a repeating pattern? That is, do the symptoms occur at the same time every day? Is the pattern periodic? Is the pattern cyclic?

Recurring Problems

Sometimes, when a process or specific piece of equipment allegedly has been repaired, the same problem recurs with exactly the same symptoms as before. Recurring problems are always the direct result of inadequate or incomplete problem-solving techniques used in the first place. Typically, recurring problems exist because of one of the following symptoms:

- The root cause of the problem was not found; therefore, only a symptom was treated.
- The repair was inadequate or incomplete.

- The diagnosis was made with insufficient or inaccurate information (maybe a trap was present) and thus was incorrect.

    a. The root cause was purposely avoided. Sometimes people avoid problems they don't know how to solve or repairs they don't know how to make. Sometimes people even avoid problems because they are too tired or lazy or don't care.

    b. The cost or time to make the repair was prohibitive, so a temporary, cheaper or quicker repair was made. We all know that cheaper repairs always cost more and quicker repairs always take longer in the final analysis, don't we?

Problem-Solving Truth #25: *The key to finding the root cause of intermittent problems is determining the timing of symptoms and then relating them to changes.*

Problem-Solving Truth #26: *Recurring problems are always the direct result of inadequate or incomplete problem-solving techniques.*

1.8 DOCUMENTATION

Once a problem has been solved, the work of the problem solver or team is not yet complete. Almost as important as solving the problem is documenting the process for future use. In fact, this is critical to long-term improvement. Problem-solving events, done correctly, become case studies

Documentation

Expected Performance
Definition/Description
Changes
Analysis
Testing
Actions Taken

that will improve problem-solving efficiency and effectiveness in the future. Envision a database that contains details of solved problems. Wouldn't that make solving the same problem quicker and more effective? Again, use a logical pathway for document procedures:

1. Compare the expected level of performance to the actual level of performance when the problem is present.
2. Following the guidelines in Section 1.4 of this chapter, develop and record a complete definition and description of the problem.
3. Detect and list all observed symptoms related to the problem.
4. Develop a complete record of all changes that occurred prior to the problem, then list all changes made by your problem-solving team.
5. Document completely the steps taken to get to the root cause. This would include an analysis of changes, distinctions, and differences found.
6. Document the hypotheses you have developed based on your analysis and the list of possible causes.
7. Document all completed tests, the criteria used to judge the results, and the final list of most probable causes. In this section, include any tools you may have used—why?-why? diagrams, cause-and-effect diagrams, charts, graphs, and so on.
8. Document the action(s) taken on the cause(s), and the results. Include any first-piece inspection test results.
9. Document the results of testing to validate that the solution was effective and didn't create other process problems.
10. Document any controls or preventive measures put in place to avoid a recurrence of the problem.

1.9 PROBLEM ASSIGNMENT

Upon concluding this chapter, complete the following assignment:

Assignment

Problem Statement
Symptoms
Changes
DFCs
Distinctions
Testing

1. Using the techniques described in this chapter, select and document an existing problem that needs to be solved on your current job. State the expected level of performance and the actual level of performance when the problem exists.

2. Using the format presented in this chapter, develop a problem statement in terms of what, where, when, how many, and any trends.

3. Using the instructions presented in this chapter, develop a complete list of symptoms, changes, etc., and then explain what you believe is the root cause of the problem and why.

4. In your own words, describe what you believe is the most probable cause and what you would do to prevent a recurrence of the problem.

What did you learn?

(In your own words, write the things you learned in this chapter and then compare them with what you should have learned.)

_____

_____

_____

_____

_____

_____

_____

_____

_____

_____

_____

_____

CHAPTER 2

Selecting the Right Problem

What You Should Learn in This Chapter

How to select the right problem to solve. What tools and techniques are available to assist in the selection of the right problem. How to use the tools to make effective decisions.

Every day, every organization is faced with a seemingly endless supply of problems to be solved. There are safety issues, quality problems, throughput problems, expense issues, personnel opportunities, and the list goes on. With all of these problems to choose from, how is one to know which one is the most important? Should we just work on the one that is receiving the most attention or the one that seems to have everyone upset? Should we work on the one that is influencing the bottom line the most? How about a customer delivery issue? Isn't that automatically the one we select? The answer is, yes! All of these factors should be considered when deciding the priority order for attack.

Many organizations simply roll up their collective sleeves, jump in with both feet, and attack all of their problems simultaneously. The end result can be chaos, a dilution of the resource base, and anxiety over the plethora of unsolved problems. The smart organizations understand that there is a hierarchy of problems in terms of importance and organizational impact and that trying to solve all of them at the same time usually results in few of them being solved at all. Selecting the priority order of problems to solve should be the result of a deliberate and systematic approach, using tools that are designed for this purpose. Every problem is a "treasure" because it represents an opportunity for the organization to improve.

Problem-Solving Truth #27: *Every problem is a treasure because it represents an opportunity for the organization to improve.*

2.1 PARETO AND PIE CHARTS

Like so many other opportunities, we should always use a systematic and deliberate approach when we are selecting our opportunities for improvement. Using a systematic approach and tools to facilitate our

Pareto/Pie Charts

Pareto Charts
Pareto Principle
80/20 Rule

decision makes the selection process so much easier and effective. One of the most common tools available for use to select and prioritize problems is the Pareto chart. It is named in honor of Vilfredo Pareto, an Italian economist who was studying the economic wealth distribution in the 19th century in Italy. Pareto discovered an interesting phenomena relating to wealth in Italy. Pareto concluded that 80 percent of his country's wealth was controlled by only 20 percent of the population.

Dr. Joseph Juran, a noted American quality guru, further developed what Pareto had inadvertently discovered and appropriately named the Pareto chart in honor of Vilfredo Pareto. The relationship or distribution that Pareto discovered, as it relates to problems, was that 80 percent of problems are manifested in 20 percent of the items with problems. This concept has since proved to be true in many other areas. For example, problems like absenteeism, accidents, defects, etc., all typically follow this "80/20 rule." That is, 80 percent of all accidents and absenteeism occur with 20 percent of the workers. The assumption behind the Pareto principle is that if you focus your effort on 20 percent of the problems, you will have fixed 80 percent of the problems. It has been my experience that this principle is true and sets the stage for selecting the right area(s) of focus.

The Pareto chart is intended to display the problems graphically in priority order from most to least frequent or most to least important. Constructing Pareto charts is a simple task in that you simply assemble the problem categories and the frequencies of each, layout the categories along the x-axis and then plot the frequencies along the y-axis. So, let's create a Pareto chart.

The example we will use was from a company producing SMC trailer panels for large Class 8 trucks. The team first collected the data to be charted that included a listing of problem areas and the frequency of occurrence of each individual area. Table 2-1 is a listing of data of defects on panels being supplied to a truck body manufacturer.

Table 2-1.

PROBLEM	FREQUENCY	% OF TOTAL
Blisters	57	75
Cracks	8	10
Pits	5	6
Holes	4	5
Mars	2	3
Blowouts	1	1

As you can see, the number one defect in terms of number of occurrences is clearly blisters. That is, of the 77 total defects observed, 57 of them were blisters. Based upon this analysis, 16.7 percent of the defects (blisters = 1/6 of the categories of defects) account for approximately 75 percent of the total number of defects. Remembering the Pareto principle, if we were to solve the blister problem (16.7 percent of the total), we would reduce the number of defects by approximately 75 percent. Close to the 80/20 rule, isn't it? The next step is to transform the raw data into graphical form by arranging the defect types along the x-axis in order of their frequency and frequency of each along the y-axis as in Figure 2-1. The traditional format for the Pareto chart is to then draw boxes with the height being dictated by the number (or percentage) of occurrence of each category (defect, in this case). Figure 2-1 is a graphical representation of the data presented in Table 2-1 and can easily be constructed using Excel or by hand.

SMC DEFECTS

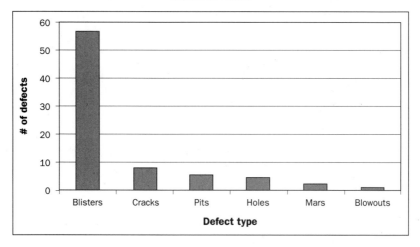

Figure 2-1.

The Pareto chart (see Figure 2-1) has provided us with the opportunity to define our area of focus in a general sense, but the subject is still a bit too vague to be of value from a problem-solving perspective. That is, just by knowing that blisters are the number one problem doesn't tell us enough about the problem to be able to begin our problem resolution activities. Even though we know that blisters are our biggest problem, we need to know where the blisters are before we can attack them. Right? Let's look deeper into this problem by further refining our blister profile.

Table 2-2 is a summary of blister data by part type and as you can see, one part in particular (J40) has a very high level of blisters when compared to the others. In fact, this part accounts for 74 percent of the total blisters.

Table 2-2.

PART TYPE	FREQUENCY	% OF TOTAL
J40	42	74
J50	7	12
J60	3	5
J70	2	4
J80	2	4
J90	1	1

Figure 2-2 is the Pareto chart of this data and as you can see, product type J40 clearly has many more blisters than any other type and should be our area of focus. This "lower level" Pareto

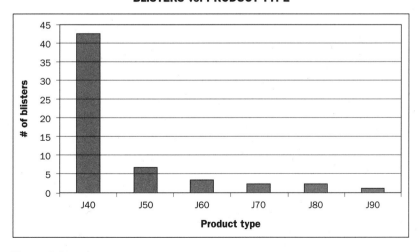

BLISTERS vs. PRODUCT TYPE

Figure 2-2.

chart has answered the question regarding where the blisters are, in terms of product type, but we need more information such as the location of these blisters. Again, we turn to an even lower level Pareto Chart to answer this question.

This team first divided the part into six zones based upon location as follows:

Zone A	Zone C	Zone E
Zone B	Zone D	Zone F

The team then inspected panels for blisters within each zone and put them in tabular form (see Table 2-3).

Table 2-3.

Location on Part	FREQUENCY	% OF TOTAL
Zone A	30	72
Zone B	5	12
Zone C	3	7
Zone D	2	5
Zone E	1	2
Zone F	1	2

As you can see, Zone A clearly contains the majority of the blisters and will be the team's area of focus.

Figure 2-3 is the graphical representation (Pareto chart) of the data from Table 2-3 and as you can see, Zone A should be the area of focus for their problem-solving activities. By using Pareto charts, the team now has a clear sense of direction—blisters on part J40 in Zone A.

There are other ways that this same information can be presented, but the outcome remains the same. For example, Figure 2-4 is the same data used in the Figure 2-1, but it is presented in the form of a pie chart. The pie chart is constructed

BLISTERS BY ZONE

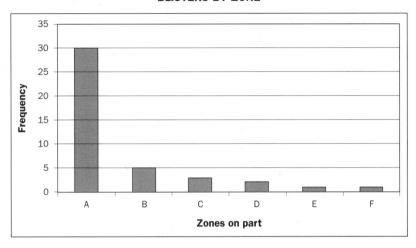

Figure 2-3.

in the same manner as the Pareto chart in that frequency data is assembled by category and the pieces of the pie are proportional to the frequency or percentage of the defect, in this case. As you can see from the pie chart, like the Pareto chart, blisters

SMC DEFECTS

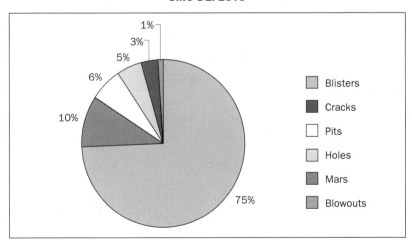

Figure 2-4.

are the number one defect and should be the focus of our attention. Like the Pareto charts, lower level pie charts can be constructed to further refine the area of focus.

The team's selection of which graphical technique to use was not important; it was the correct conclusion of which area to focus on that was important. The defect profile or area of focus should be on blisters on product J40 in Zone A. We might have reached the same conclusion simply by talking to people and viewing parts with the problem, but Pareto charts plainly justify our selection.

2.2 PROBLEM IMPACT MATRIX

If you've ever been involved in a "turnaround," then you know that your problems are of a larger scope than simply defects or safety problems. Everywhere you turn there are areas of improvement that impact

Problem Impact Matrix
Turnaround
Impact criteria
Ratings
Problem Impact Number

your bottom line. In addition to process problems, systems problems limit your organization's ability to function. How do you know which issues to address or which problems to focus on?

One tool that I have used over the years is called the Problem Impact Matrix. This matrix is used to evaluate a variety of issues by using predetermined criteria to rate each issue's impact on the organization. The ratings are then multiplied times each other to get a Problem Impact Number (PIN). The higher the PIN, the more it has an impact on the organization. Therefore, the highest PINs should be selected as issues to assign to a problem-solving team to correct. The selected criteria vary, but typically include the following:

1. Impact on the bottom line?
2. Impact on quality?
3. Impact on throughput?
4. Impact on delivery?
5. Impact on safety?

This technique can be used to evaluate a wide variety of issues, so other criteria could be substituted as desired.

A typical Problem Impact Matrix looks like Table 2-4 as follows:

Table 2-4.

PROBLEM IMPACT MATRIX					
Evaluation Criteria					
Problem/ Issues	Bottom Line $ Impact	Quality Impact	Safety Impact	Throughput or Delivery Impact	PIN

The matrix contains a column for listing the problems or issues and typically 3 to 4 criteria used to evaluate/rate the problem in terms of its impact on the organization. Finally, the matrix contains a column for recording the PIN.

The rating scale used to evaluate each of the individual criteria is typically three numbers that relate to low, medium, and high in terms of impact on the organization. I recommend that you provide enough spacing between these numbers so as to be able to differentiate the results. For example, if you used (1) for low impact, (2) for medium impact, and (3) for high impact, you could end up with all of the problems having similar PINs and the decision on which problem to address would be more difficult. For this same reason, I recommend multiplying the criteria rather than adding the individual values. Therefore, my recommended rating scale is as follows:

Rating Scale
1 = Low Impact   5 = Medium Impact   10 = High Impact

Let's look at an example. The leadership of a manufacturing plant that produces truck bodies for the Class 3-7 truck market had several difficult problems that needed to be addressed: it had a quality issue (blisters in 20 percent of their parts as received from their supplier); one of the riveting presses was shut down for mechanical issues and was unable to produce parts; there was an electrical problem (a short in the wiring) that was raising a serious safety issue; the absenteeism rate was excessive; and the process waste was extremely high. Faced with these issues, the management team was attempting to solve all of the problems at the same time and was in a state of chaos, not solving any of the issues. It needed to step back and systematically look at all of these issues and make an intelligent decision

PROBLEM IMPACT MATRIX					
Evaluation Criteria					
Problem/ Issues	Bottom Line $ Impact	Quality Impact	Safety Impact	Throughput or Delivery Impact	PIN
Blisters in 20 percent of parts	7	8	1	8	448
Press shut down	6	2	1	10	120
Electrical short	1	1	10	8	80
Absenteeism rate is excessive	7	7	1	9	441
Process waste is excessive	9	1	1	1	9

Figure 2-5.

on which problems to tackle. The team chose the Problem Impact Matrix with the results summarized in Figure 2-5.

In Figure 2-5, five separate issues were evaluated for impact on the bottom line, impact on quality, impact on safety, and impact on throughput and/or delivery. Based upon this evaluation, the team believed that both blisters and absenteeism had the potential to impact the organization the most. They created two teams, one for each issue, and were able to solve both problems. By using the Problem Impact Matrix, the team was able to select the right problems to address without diluting the organization's resources and did not rely on things like emotion or the bosses' "pick of the day."

2.3 PROBLEM ASSIGNMENT

As soon as possible after having read this chapter, complete the following assignment:

Assignment

Problem Impact Matrix
Pareto Chart
Pie Chart

1. Using the techniques learned in this chapter, create a problem impact matrix and select a problem/issue.
2. Using the techniques learned in this chapter, create a Pareto chart with multiple levels on the above problem.
3. Using the techniques learned in this chapter and using the same problem above, create a pie chart.

What did you learn?

(In your own words, write the things you learned in this chapter and then compare them with what you should have learned.)

_____

_____

_____

_____

_____

_____

_____

_____

_____

_____

_____

_____

_____

CHAPTER 3

Problem-Solving Teams

What You Should Learn in This Chapter

How to select the correct members for a problem-solving team. What the role of the team leader is. What the role of the team members is. What brainstorming is and how to use it.

Although most people personally enjoy taking credit for solving problems, rarely do individuals actually account for all the actions in a problem-solving event. This doesn't mean that individuals can't solve a problem by themselves, but usually they have received some form of assistance from someone along the problem-solving pathway. An explanation from a maintenance mechanic on how a piece of equipment functions; an analysis of data from a statistician; operating instructions from a machine operator; an answer to a design question from an engineer—all of these subtle actions were probably important pieces to the problem-solving puzzle. If you are an individualist or get your own personal high from solving problems by riding in on your white horse and proclaiming "Problem solved!," then you should stop, get off your horse, and smell the coffee—because you need help!

One thing that troubles me is that many people still hang on to the outdated belief that quality and equipment problems are the responsibility of the quality and maintenance departments. This belief is so far from reality and current-day thinking. Problems are everyone's responsibility and, as such, solving

43

problems should be a team event. Effective problem-solving events are the synergistic result of a functionally diverse team using a structured approach. Think about it, how much can one person know? It is always a good idea to use a team approach to solve problems.

Problem-Solving Truth #28: *Effective problem solving is the synergistic result of a functionally diverse team using a structured approach.*

- In this chapter, we will focus on:
- The make-up of the problem-solving team.
- The role of the team leader.
- The role of the team members.
- How to generate ideas through brainstorming.
- An assignment to practice what we have learned.

3.1 THE PROBLEM-SOLVING TEAM

So, if using a team is a better way to solve problems, then what should the team look like? That is, what functional groups should be represented and what specific roles should be active members of the team? If you, for example, are in a manufacturing

The Team
Operations
Maintenance/Tooling
Quality/Engineering
Cross-Functional

environment, then my recommendation is that you include team members from at least three distinct plant functions. Figure 3-1 describes these three functions. The process owner is the function or person authorized to make the final decisions on the process. The support groups are those functions that have clear responsibility to the process, like technical expertise or material flow, but aren't given change authority.

In the case of a manufacturing unit, Figure 3-2 describes the potential team players. These three functions — Opera-

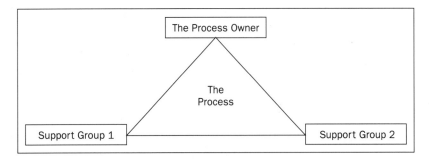

Figure 3-1.

tions, Maintenance and Tooling, and Quality and Engineering—usually have all of the information needed to solve most manufacturing problems.

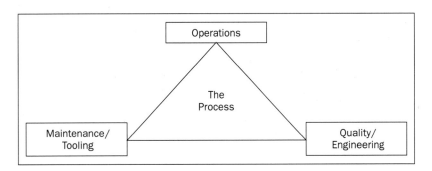

Figure 3-2.

All three functions have a vested interest in the process with the problem with Operations being the process owner and the other two being support groups. In this case, Quality and Engineering's function is to supply technical direction regarding design intent, process optimization, etc., while Tooling and Maintenance is charged with assuring the performance and optimization of the process equipment.

The team should also be aware of the need for functional experts as they are needed and should actively recruit them when their skills are considered necessary. Suppose data had to be analyzed and no one on the team had the necessary skills to do so. The team might recruit a statistician for this specific function. What if the team had a material or a financial question? The team must always be aware of this potential need and solicit the input of a temporary team member as required.

Specifically, who from each of these functions should be on the problem-solving team? Personally, I have always tried to involve the people who are normally closest to the process as members of the team. That includes machine operators, maintenance workers (e.g., millwrights, electricians), engineers, and supervisors. It still amazes me how often machine operators are not included on problem-solving teams. After all that has been written about operator involvement, teams often include only management people! *People who may never have run the equipment with the problem are on the team!* In the end, the membership on the problem-solving team should be limited to people with vested interest in the process with the problem! The people who will benefit most when the problem is solved are the people who should be charged with solving it.

Finally, how big should the team be? It has been my experience that the size of the core team should be no more than five to six people including the team leader. Teams larger than six have a tendency to get bogged down with trivial things. I recommend that the team be cross-functional and should consist of the leader, the machine operator, an electrician, a mechanic or millwright, and an engineer (or their functional equivalents in other disciplines).

Problem-Solving Truth #29: *Membership on a problem-solving team should be limited to people who have a vested interest in the process with the problem.*

3.2 THE TEAM LEADER

Much has been written about the role of the team leader, but the leader is simply the person who manages the activities of the team. Many times, the team leader is a supervisor of the process with the problem, but,

The Team Leader
Manages
Communications Conduit
Motivating
Teaching/Coaching

quite frankly, my experience tells me that not all supervisors make good leaders or facilitators. If this is the case, then other arrangements must be made in terms of who leads the team.

The team leader has a variety of duties and responsibilities to the team. The leader schedules and facilitates the team meetings, handles any administrative details, and acts as the communications conduit for the team. More importantly though, the team leader is responsible for directing, involving, motivating, teaching, and coaching the team members to stay on course until the problem is resolved. With these responsibilities in mind, make sure that the selection of the team leader is done with much thought and that the team leader has received appropriate problem-solving training.

3.3 THE TEAM MEMBERS

The team members are all responsible for assuring that the problem gets properly investigated, analyzed, and ultimately solved in a timely manner and, as such, all members must actively participate toward that end. Team members are responsible for sharing their

The Team Members
Sharing Knowledge
Participating
Assignments
Documenting
Communicating

knowledge, expertise and ideas, participating during team

meetings, carrying out their individual assignments between meetings, and documenting their findings. This last point—documentation—is extremely important not only for the problem-solving event that the team is involved with, but for future use by others of the team's findings. So many times I have seen teams come together and solve problems, but by failing to document their findings properly, they fail to develop an important piece of history for their company.

The team members, especially if they are hourly operators, have an added responsibility to the long-term eradication of the problem they are solving. Once the solution and the preventive measures are put in place, someone must communicate to those who weren't a member of the team. I have always believed that this is the job of the machine operators who were a part of the team. Ultimately, the long-term success or failure of a problem-solving event lies in the hands of the machine operators. Who relates better to machine operators than other machine operators?

3.4 BRAINSTORMING

Many times, the problems we are trying our best to solve as individuals require the input and assistance of our peers. Because we need this input, we need a way to bring together all of the necessary information to

> **Brainstorming**
> Problem Resolution Plan
> Creative Thinking
> Free-Thinking
> Promotes Teamwork

create a coherent problem resolution plan. One of the easiest and most enjoyable ways to develop this plan is to brainstorm. Brainstorming is a technique that facilitates and stimulates creative thinking. It is based upon the premise that one idea stimulates another and requires no formal training prior to implementation. Brainstorming is one of the best tools available to create a sense of involvement and participation of the team members and truly sets the stage for action. So how does brainstorming work?

First, the topic or problem to be solved must be as specific as possible. Suppose the topic to be brainstormed was a quality defect called pinholes, sometimes seen in fiberglass parts. Instead of the topic to be brainstormed being quality defects, it would be better to define the topic as "possible failure modes that create pinholes." The topic to be brainstormed should be given to the people who will be involved in the brainstorming in advance so that they have time to develop a list of ideas on the subject.

There are several rules of action or guidelines that must be established and agreed upon prior to beginning the brain-storming session if it is to be successful.

1. The leader or facilitator of the brainstorming session must maintain some sense of order and avoid a verbal free-for-all, but at the same time must encourage a freethinking exchange of information. That is, instead of chaos, there must be a systematic approach used to obtain input from the brainstormers.

2. Starting with one person, each member takes his or her turn in order, with only one idea being given at a time. Using our pinhole example with four people, some of the ideas from the session might look like this:
   Person 1: Out-of-age catalyst
   Person 2: High fluid pressure
   Person 3: Hot mold
   Person 4: Short outgas time
   Person 1: Gelcoat not mixed
   Person 2: Too high catalyst percent
   The session continues until there are no more ideas to record. Remember that the ideas generated are potential causes of the problem being brainstormed.

3. No idea is ever criticized!!! All ideas may have merit, but even if they don't, don't criticize them because it will stifle the creativity of the group!
4. All ideas should be recorded for the team to see on something like a flip chart or chalkboard. Visibility stimulates creativity.
5. If a participant doesn't have an idea, he or she may pass until his or her next turn.
6. The process continues until all ideas are exhausted or until everyone has passed. A typical brainstorming session usually takes 20 to 30 minutes to complete, depending upon the complexity of the problem being discussed and the size of the group.

Brainstorming, as a technique, has several important benefits that ultimately helps in the problem-solving process as follows:

1. A significant number of ideas or potential causes of the problem will result.
2. Brainstorming stimulates creative ideas.
3. Brainstorming breaks down narrow-minded perceptions of the problem being discussed.
4. Brainstorming promotes, enhances, and reinforces the concept of teamwork and participation.

3.5 MAKING THINGS HAPPEN

Once the brainstorming session has ended, the team must now take the ideas generated and turn them into qualitative actions to correct the problem. In order to accomplish this effectively, the team must develop a plan of action that clearly lists the actions, some form of a timeline, who is responsible for making sure the actions are completed, and the status of the action item. This plan can take a variety of different formats, but my recommendation is to keep it simple. One simple format is demonstrated in Table 3-1 below.

Making Things Happen

Action Plan

Actions

Timeline

Responsibilities

Simple

Reviews

Having a plan in place is not the end of the event for the problem-solving team. I can't tell you how many times I have seen action plans developed and presented only to see the plan not executed. It's almost as though the action plan is the end product! Based upon my experiences, the single biggest reason for plans not being completed is the lack of involvement of management in the review process. Plan, Do, Check, Act (PDCA) is not just a collection of words, it is a logical sequence of events for making things happen. The Check portion relates to reviewing the action plan at regular intervals to determine the status and to assure that progress is being made. Without these regular reviews plans usually are not completed, so make sure your plan is a living document. One way to do this is to develop a schedule of future reviews.

Table 3-1.

Action Item	Start Date	End Date Date	Responsible	Status/ Comments

3.6 PROBLEM ASSIGNMENT

As soon as possible after completion of this chapter, complete the following assignment:

> **Assignment**
> Form Team
> Present Problem
> Brainstorm
> List of Potential Causes
> Develop Action Plan
> Review Action Plan

1. Form a team using the guidelines presented in Section 3.1.
2. Present the problem selected in Chapter 1's assignment to the team.
3. Using the guidelines in Section 3.4, hold a brainstorming session to generate and record (write) potential causes to the problem.
4. Using the guidelines in Section 3.5, develop an action plan that contains action steps, start and completion dates, and status.
5. In order to assure regular reviews of your plan, establish a review schedule.

What did you learn?

(In your own words, write the things you learned in this chapter and then compare them with what you should have learned.)

_____

_____

_____

_____

_____

_____

_____

_____

_____

_____

_____

_____

_____

_____

CHAPTER 4
The Why?-Why? Tools in Problem Solving

What You Should Learn in This Chapter

What Cause and Effect Diagrams, Why?-Why? Diagrams, Tree Diagrams, and Causal Chains are, how to construct them, and how to use them to solve problems.

Effective problem solving is always the direct result of knowing which tools to use and when to use them. There are many different tools that can and should be used, but, in my opinion, some are better or more effective than others. For example, if you are in the midst of a major quality improvement effort, then you will want some kind of tool that helps you prioritize your selection of issues and problems. The Pareto chart is an excellent choice. If your objective is to optimize process settings or to determine which process factors significantly affect your process, then a Designed Experiment is your tool of choice.

In this chapter, I have assumed that you already know what problem you will be solving and you are ready to go forward in your problem-solving activities. The four tools presented in this chapter all ask the question Why as a means of learning more about the problem and finding the potential root causes.

In this chapter we will focus on:

1. The cause and effect diagrams
2. The why?-why? diagrams

3. The tree diagrams
4. The causal chains

These four tools are simple to learn and use and are very effective in your search for the root cause(s) of the problem.

4.1 THE CAUSE AND EFFECT DIAGRAM

One of the most popular and widely used problem-solving tools available is the cause and effect (C&E) diagram. C&E diagrams were developed by Dr. Kaoru Ishikawa, a noted Japanese consultant and author of *Guide to Quality Control*.[2] They have been used successfully by teams around the

Cause and Effect

Fishbone
Man
Methods
Materials
Machines

world. In honor of Dr. Ishikawa, this tool is sometimes referred to as an Ishikawa diagram, but it is also referred to as a fishbone diagram because its basic structure resembles the skeleton of a fish. Whatever you wish to call them, a cause and effect diagram is a useful tool that must be a part of the problem solver's toolkit.

The C&E diagram shown below (see Figure 4-1) is used to develop and organize potential causes of a problem. The potential causes are listed on the fishbones driving toward the problem (effect). The effect or problem is stated to the right while the potential causes are listed on the fishbones to the left under the appropriate category headings. By arranging lists in this manner, there is often a greater understanding of the problem and possible contributing factors.

Typical C & E diagrams are constructed with four major categories of potential causes (4 Ms: Man, Method, Materials, and Machines), but the C & E diagram should be custom-fitted to the needs of the user. In other words, other categories can be added to further organize the potential causes. In the

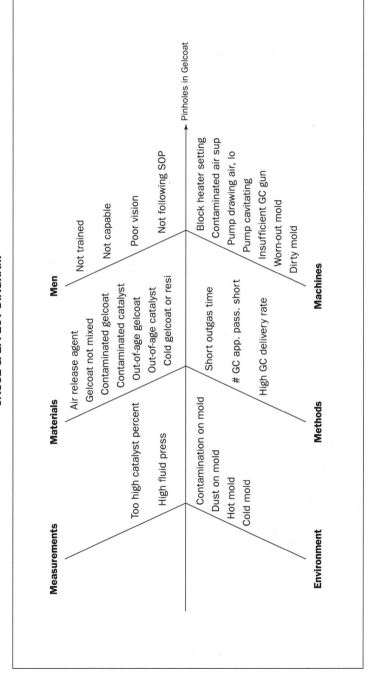

CAUSE & EFFECT DIAGRAM

Figure 4-1.

example above, two additional categories (Environment and Measurement) have been added.

In this example, the team was attempting to solve a pinhole problem on a fiberglass part. The team simply stated the problem as Pinholes in Gelcoat, and then brainstormed to develop a list of potential causes. The steps in creating and using a fishbone are as follows (Appendix C contains a blank C & E Diagram for the reader to use and copy):

1. Develop a statement of the problem which describes the problem in terms of what it is, where it is occurring, when it is occurring, and how extensive it is. This statement is the effect and is listed to the right on the fishbone diagram. In our example, the problem was simply listed as pinholes in gelcoat. The team had developed and posted a more complete problem statement, but for the sake of brevity, they simply stated the problem as pinholes.

2. Brainstorm and create a list of causal categories that will be used to develop the possible causes on the C & E diagram. If the problem was equipment related, our categories might be listed as Electrical, Mechanical, Pneumatic, Man, Methods, and Material. The team must be creative when selecting the causal categories.

3. Construct the C & E diagram by:
   a. Placing the problem statement to the right of the fishbones.
   b. Listing the causal categories above and below the fishbones.
   c. Brainstorming and listing the possible causes on the fishbones under the appropriate causal category heading.

4. Interpret the C & E diagram by:

a. Looking for causes listed in the individual fishbones and testing the potential causes to determine if they have an impact on the effect.
b. Gathering additional data and information to validate the potential causes.

A variation of the above technique is to ask Why after each cause is listed and then expand the fishbone with additional branches (see Figure 4-2). For example, suppose the problem was a hydraulic press that had stopped functioning and one of the causal categories was "electrical." On the first bone, we might have listed "motor stopped." If we ask why the motor stopped, we may have concluded that the current stopped. Why did the current stop? The switch had opened. We continue asking why and create new fishbones until we understand the potential cause.

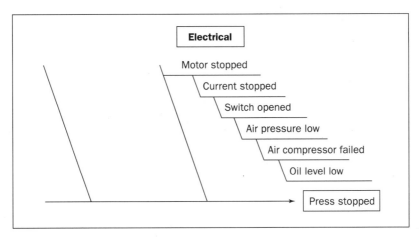

Figure 4-2.

Remember, like all problem-solving tools, the C&E diagram will only identify possible causes. Only data and other information about the causes will lead you to the actual root cause(s).

4.2 THE WHY?-WHY? DIAGRAM

If you're in the market for a great method that helps you organize your thinking, then the why?-why? diagram just might be the tool for you. Why?-why diagrams were developed in the early 1980s[3] in work associated with

> **Why?-Why? Diagrams**
>
> Diagram
> Branches
> Materials
> Machines

quality circles and are equally useful in both production and administrative environments.

A why?-why? diagram, as seen in Figure 4-3, like most other problem-solving tools, begins with a statement of the problem to be solved and asks the question Why.

The problem-solving team then responds to the Why question and develops potential cause statements that are believed to be creating the problem. For example, if a plant was working on a problem of "Bending process receiving cold parts," then the first two answers to the Why question might be:

1. Too much time from the oven to the bending process.
2. The parts are cold coming out of the oven.

After each of these questions, we would then ask Why again. We would repeat this procedure until we could no longer ask Why (i.e., we have arrived at the potential root cause). The completed why?-why? diagram (see Figure 4-3) continues to expand this procedure. As we move from left to right answering our new Why questions, we create branches that sometimes contain multiple questions to be answered. The cause statements to the right now become new problems statements, and the process continues.

As we continue to ask Why, we develop a network of reasons why the original problem on the left occurred. When we arrive at a logical conclusion or we perform a test or check, we simply stop and move to the next level of the why?-why? diagram.

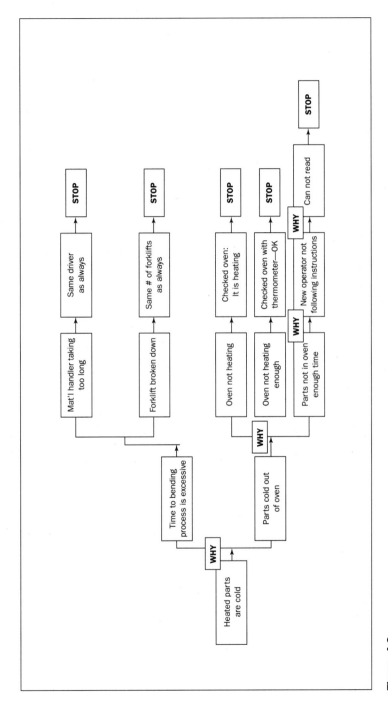

Figure 4-3.

The completed why?-why? diagram is really nothing more than a logic diagram that outlines the elements of a systematic approach to resolving a problem. Again, the elements that were originally defined as causes to the problem to their right become new problems that have their own causes. In our example, the ultimate solution to why parts were being received cold was to hire a new operator or teach the existing operator how to follow instructions without reading. A longer-term solution might be to automate the baking step.

The why?-why? diagram is an effective tool that helps the problem-solving team arrive at a solution. It pulls together a picture of the method used to solve the problem and then becomes an excellent presentation tool. The why?-why? diagram also brings a new level of understanding to both problems situations and the process or system with the problem.

4.3 THE TREE DIAGRAM

Another tool that can be used to assist with problem-solving efforts is the tree diagram, so named because it utilizes a branching effect. Tree diagrams were developed by the Japanese and are basically tools that facilitate the devel-

Tree Diagram
How? or What?
Branches
Action Plans

opment of specific action plans to solve problems or achieve goals. The tree diagram (see Figure 4-4) is created in much the same way as the why?-why? diagram in that you begin by stating the problem (or goal to achieve) on the left side of the diagram. Instead of asking Why, like we do in the why?-why? diagram, we ask "how can this problem be overcome?" or "what issues must be addressed to solve this problem?"

Like the C&E and why?-why? diagrams, the tree diagram provides us with a structured approach that ensures a linkage between problems and solutions. Once these questions have

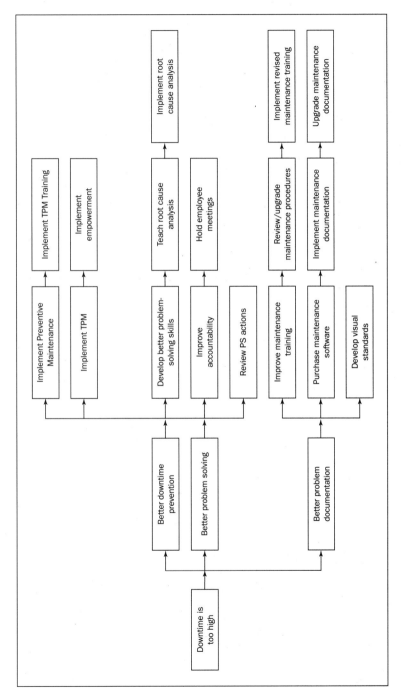

Figure 4-4.

been answered, we then ask the question, "Can I solve the problem or achieve the goal as stated?" If we can't answer yes, then we must develop another branch (level) of the tree. We then ask, "Will the specific action outlined resolve the problem or achieve the goal?" If not, then we continue to the next branch and so on. The process continues until the tree is complete and then a list of specific actions is developed (i.e., a plan). If the process was done correctly, and if the actions are implemented according to the plan, then the problem will be solved or the goal will be achieved. The final branches on the tree diagram should be the specific actions to take.

The example in Figure 4-4 involves the development of a plan to address excessive levels of equipment downtime. The problem-solving team chose three separate general actions in the first branch of the tree diagram:

1. Better downtime prevention to avoid scraps in the first place.
2. Better problem solving to limit the amount of downtime.
3. Better maintenance documentation

The final actions to be taken involve training in continuous improvement (i.e., TPM training), empowerment, root cause analysis, and maintenance documentation as well as developing maintenance software. The completed tree diagram on the previous page is an example of an easy-to-use guide to solving a problem or achieving a goal.

The tree diagram is a valuable tool for translating problems or goals into specific action items. The important ingredients for creating a useful tree diagram are for the problem-solving team to have either a knowledge of the process(es) involved or to be able to facilitate a group discussion on the subject at hand. Ultimately, the problem-solving team must identify the direct cause and effect relationships that exist between each branch of the tree.

4.4 CAUSAL CHAINS

When problems are discovered and investigated, a chain of events always lead to the problem source or the root cause. One of the most effective techniques for uncovering the root cause of the problem is the causal chain or, as they are

> **Causal Chains**
>
> Chain of Events
> Chains of Causality
> Steps/Sawtooth
> Object/State

sometimes referred to, chains of causality. Causal chains are stepwise evolutions of problem causes. Causal chains are typically seen in two different chain-like patterns as depicted in Figure 4-5.

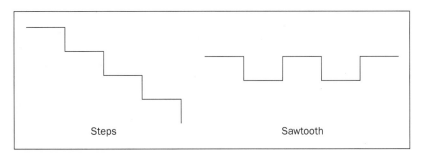

Steps   Sawtooth

Figure 4-5.

Each step (or sawtooth) represents an object in a normal or abnormal state. The object is placed above the step line and its state is placed below the line, directly underneath the object. Some examples of objects and states might be:

Object	State
Fuel line	Plugged
Circuit Breaker	Tripped
Tire	Flat
Motor	Stopped

Each step (or sawtooth) is the cause of the next step and the effect of the preceding step. That is, the information on the step to the left is always the cause of the information on the step to the right. Figure 4-6 is an example of a completed causal chain for a punch press that stopped for no apparent reason.

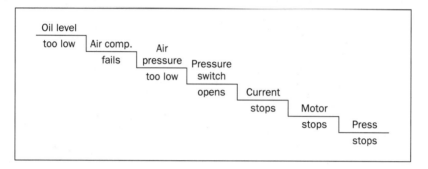

Figure 4-6.

An investigation of the problem reveals that a pressure switch had tripped the circuit breaker to the press's electric motor. In this example, we start with the problem symptom (the punch press had stopped), and continue in a stepwise direction to the left by asking Why until we arrive at the root cause of the problem. The punch press had stopped because the motor had stopped because the current to the motor stopped because the pressure switch had opened because the pressure was too low because the air compressor had failed because the oil level was low. Causal chains are simply logical steps from the problem symptom to the cause or causes. They are, in fact, the chain of events that created the problem.

To take this example even further, suppose we had two punch presses that used the same air compressor. If this were the case, then the causal chains for each punch press would be identical but would be joined at the common source of the problem, the compressed air lines (see Figure 4-7). Remember what we said earlier about having symptoms that occur at the same time: Simultaneous symptoms have common causes. The example below shows how this might appear. Since both presses stopped for the same reason, then the causal chains are joined at the problem source.

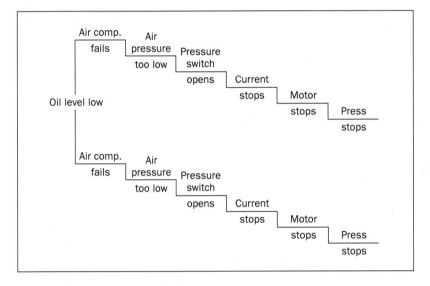

Figure 4-7.

One additional technique sometimes used in conjunction with causal chains is the addition of a diagonal line at the elbow of the step to indicate a deviation from the normal state. That is, the diagonal indicates that the object is in an abnormal state. Each step with a deviation would look like Figure 4-8.

Problem Solving Truth #30: *When problems are discovered and investigated, a chain of events always lead to the problem source or root cause.*

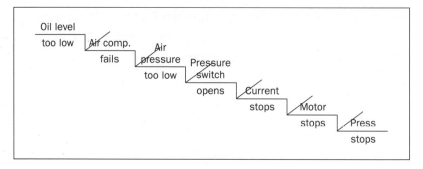

Figure 4-8.

4.5 PROBLEM ASSIGNMENT

As soon as possible, after completion of this chapter, complete the following assignment:

> **Assignment**
> Cause & Effect Diagram
> Why?-Why? Diagram
> Causal Chain

1. Develop (draw) a C&E diagram for the problem that you selected as an assignment in Section 1.9.
2. Develop (draw) a why?-why? diagram on the above problem.
3. Develop (draw) a tree diagram on a systems problem that you know exists.
4. Develop (draw) a causal chain for the problem you selected in the first two problems above.

What did you learn?

(In your own words, write the things you learned in this chapter and then compare them with what you should have learned.)

_____

_____

_____

_____

_____

_____

_____

_____

_____

_____

_____

_____

_____

CHAPTER 5

The Inquisition Tools

What You Should Learn in This Chapter

What flow charts, run charts, check sheets, and scattergrams are, how to construct them, and how to use them effectively in problem solving. Why it's so important to put data in production order before you graph and analyze it. How to determine if two variables have a cause and effect relationship and how strong the relationship is.

In addition to the why?-why? tools introduced in Chapter 4, additional tools are available to aid the problem-solving team in its quest to better understand and solve the problem. For example, knowing and understanding the sequence of steps in the process with the problem is also an essential activity in the problem-solving process. The process flow chart (or flow chart or flow diagram) facilitates this understanding. Understanding how the process is performing as a function of time is also valuable information for the team. The run chart and check sheet fill this void. Sometimes it might be necessary to determine if two variables are related or have a cause and effect relationship. Scattergrams can answer this question. In this chapter, we will learn about:

1. Flow charts
2. Run charts
3. Check sheets
4. Scattergrams

5.1 THE FLOW CHART

In Chapter 1, we said that problems were deviations in performance without a known cause or solution. One of the tools that will help identify and understand the actual and expected performance of a process so that

> **Flow Chart**
>
> Symbols
> Pictorial Representation
> Arrows and Flow Lines
> Process Steps

the deviation can be better understood is the flow chart.

A flow chart is a technique used to display a pictorial representation of the process by using symbols to indicate various types of process activities. It is used to determine how individual steps in a process are interrelated and how a process is actually running, compared to how it should be running. In order for a flow chart to be useful, it must be constructed after thoroughly observing how the process is running over time. It cannot and must not be constructed based upon how you think or hope it is running. I have witnessed teams construct flow charts based upon memory, in an office, and the end product is usually incorrect. It is important to remember that processes are usually dynamic and change regularly. Unless you observe them over a period of time, your flow chart will be wrong. If your operation runs over a three-shift schedule, then you might expect to see three different processes, that is, different methods of operation. This is especially true in labor-intensive processes. By studying a completed flow chart, it is possible to locate both the actual deviations and, as a preventive measure, potential problems with the process.

Flow charts are normally comprised of specific symbols connected by arrows and flow lines, with each symbol representing a specific step in the process. Some of these symbols are the following:

1. The origin and the endpoint are typically represented by horizontal ovals.

2. Any transformation, movements, and steps are symbolized with rectangles.
3. All decision steps (e.g., inspections) are pictured as diamonds with alternative paths tracked with flow lines.
4. Parallelograms typically represent movement (i.e., inputs or outputs), circles designate connectors to demonstrate routes entering or exiting the process, and semicircles to prevent the flow lines from crossing. A typical flow chart might look like Figure 5-1.

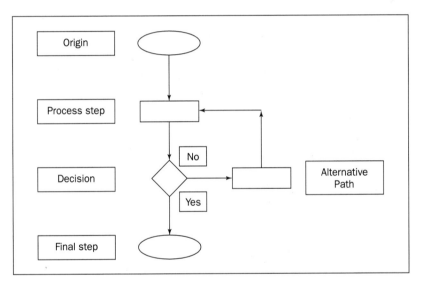

Figure 5-1.

If you are constructing a flow chart, it is important to keep it simple. You're not trying to impress anyone, you're just trying to understand the process with the problem. If you have feedback loops (e.g., diamonds), then make sure the escape routes go somewhere. For example, if the feedback loop is an inspection point, then the decision might be acceptable or unacceptable and the escape routes are either the next process step (yes) or a repair route (no). Finally, make sure you clearly define the boundaries of the process. The flow chart is a useful tool for understanding just how the process operates.

Problem-Solving Truth #31: *Most processes are dynamic and changing so it is important to study them over time. This is especially true with labor-intensive processes.*

5.2 THE RUN CHART

The performance of the process as a function of time is extremely important for two reasons.

> **Run Chart**
>
> Time
> Data Trends
> Improvement Baseline
> Effect of Changes

1. Data plotted as a function of time provide a coherent baseline of what is actually happening from a quality, throughput, or safety perspective.
2. By arranging data as a function of time (i.e., in production order), the team is clearly able to observe the effect of changes made on the process.

Run charts are both the simplest tool to construct and yet the most effective tool available to display trends of data over time. These data-over-time concepts are important for the team because it lets them visually observe the impact of both intentional and unintentional changes to the process. As data are collected, they are plotted on a graph in the order they were taken. From a problem-solving perspective, it is so important to view measurements or defects on parts produced in the order the parts were made. Let's look at some examples.

Suppose the team was working on a thickness problem (say, too thick, i.e., USL = 4.2 mm) associated with tread rubber on a tire. The team collects data on the process as it is currently running and plots the data in graphical form in Figure 5-2.

TREAD RUBBER THICKNESS vs. TIME

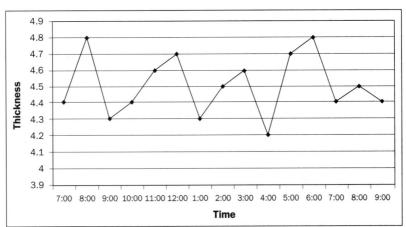

Figure 5-2.

As the team reviews the plotted data (i.e., individual data points versus time), several important observations are made:

1. All but one data point collected are at or below the upper limit of the thickness specification, i.e., 4.2 mm.
2. The average thickness of the tread rubber is approximately 4.5 mm. That is, just by "eyeballing" the data, we can estimate the process average.
3. It appears as though the data are following some sort of up and down pattern that may or may not be significant or important to finding the root cause.

Run charts can be used for a variety of different applications and can be constructed using individual data points or averages. My personal recommendation is to plot averages of data points, since individual data points include all variation inherent in the process. If the team reacts to individual data points, they might overreact to apparent shifts in data. If, on the other hand, averages shift up or down, then the shift is probably real and either requires the attention of the team or indicates that the change it made may have significantly had an impact on the process under study. By plotting averages the team gets a truer picture of what the process is doing.

Suppose the team had plotted averages (of two points) instead of individual data points. The plotted data might look like Figure 5-3.

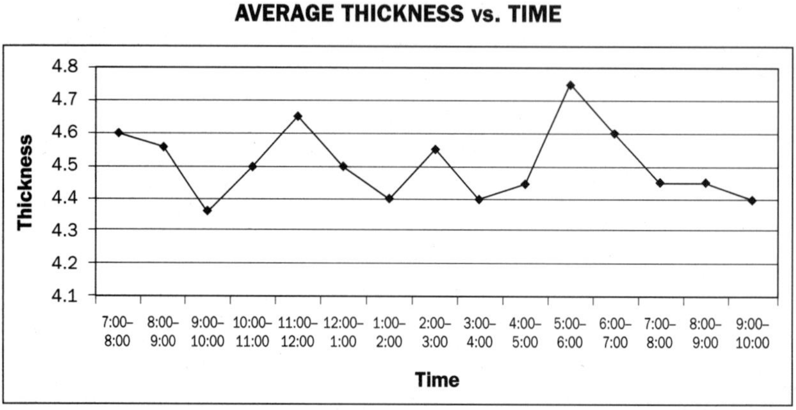

AVERAGE THICKNESS vs. TIME

Figure 5-3.

What observations might the team had made now?

1. There is no question that the average part thickness is above the upper limit of the thickness specification, i.e., too thick.
2. The wild swings in product thickness are not present, but one average (6:00–7:00) does appear to be significantly thicker than the rest and could be a focus for the team.
3. The up and down pattern is not so predominant and is probably not significant. Should the team still investigate it? They probably should.

Let's look at one more example of how a run chart can be used effectively to determine the root cause of a problem.

I was called to assist a problem-solving team working on a porosity problem on a fiberglass part produced for a major truck supplier. Porosity (small, microscopic air voids) is an age-old problem in the fiberglass industry and is difficult to detect until the part is painted and baked at the customer's location. The team investigated the problem, listed all known changes, and determined that the porosity was in the primer under the painted surface. The team had plotted the number of parts with porosity as a function of date primed. Their run chart is seen in Figure 5-4.

Since the team knew it had changed primers (i.e., DuPont 373 Primer to 1220 Primer), it had concluded that the root cause of the problem was, in fact, the new primer. After I reviewed the data, I asked the question, "If the 1220 primer was the source of the problem, then why do you still have two parts with porosity after the change from 1220 to 373 primer on November 2nd?" The team was perplexed. The team plotted the data in production order (see Figure 5-5), by shift, and an important discovery was made. All but one of the parts with porosity had been primed on the second shift! The team then audited the process closely on both the first and second shifts and discovered that the first shift was thinning the primer with acetone, while the second shift was using a reducer. The acetone had apparently been acting much like dry gas does when removing water from gasoline in your car and had removed condensation from the primer.

The team had learned several valuable problem-solving lessons. By constructing a run chart with enough detail (i.e., separate curves for the first and second shifts and in the order the parts were primed), it learned that there were process differences between the two shifts. (Notice how it recorded changes directly on the run chart.) The team also learned that by observing a defect-free configuration (i.e., first shift), they were able to detect shift-to-shift differences or distinctions in primer thinning

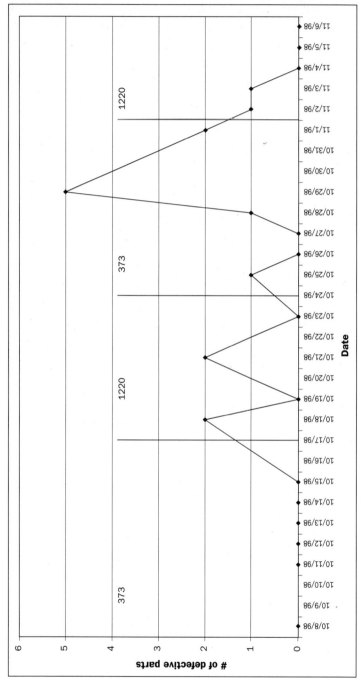

POROSITY vs. TIME

Figure 5-4.

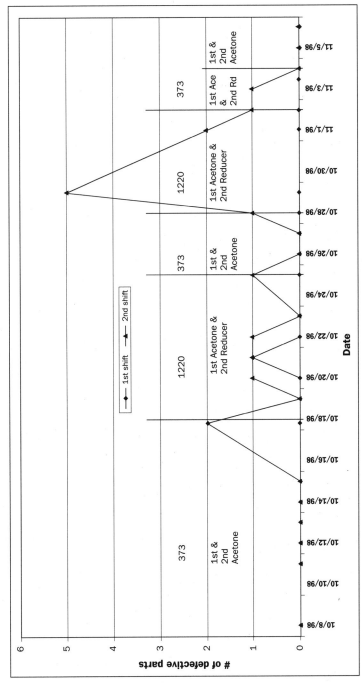

Figure 5-5.

methods. These two changes, the change in primer types and the change in primer thinning methods, were the changes responsible for the deviation in performance or the problem. As a result, the team also learned that it is possible to have multiple root causes of problems.

Run charts, if used correctly, are powerful, yet simple tools that serve problem-solving teams well.

Problem-Solving Truth #32: *When plotting data using time as an x-axis, always put the data in production order before plotting.*

Note: A blank run chart is available in Appendix C for the reader to use and copy.

5.3 CHECK SHEETS

One thing about solving problems — everyone has his or her own opinion about what the cause is. Opinions, however, aren't facts and facts are what ultimately lead to the root causes of problems. Earlier in Section 1.6 (Potential Problem-Solving Traps), we discussed the existence of potential traps that sometimes lead problem-solving efforts in the wrong direction. One of these traps was erroneous information supplied by someone involved in the process. In Section 1.7, we discussed intermittent problems and the need to document information and facts. The check sheet is a valuable tool that facilitates the collection of facts and information relative to the problem(s) being investigated.

Check Sheets
Identifiers
Classifiers
Picture Sheet
Repeating Patterns

Check sheets are simple tools that are typically used to organize and pinpoint what the problem is, when the problem is occurring, and how many times the symptoms of the problem occur. It answers the question, "How often and when are specific events happening?" In addition, the check sheet can be used to determine the trend of the problem being studied. Check sheets are, in fact, excellent data collection tools.

Check sheets come in different forms. One example is a table type check sheet that lists the identifiers (e.g., problems, symptoms, defects) in the left-hand column and has some sort of time reference in the remaining columns. Each time the symptom (or problem) is observed, a tick mark is placed in the appropriate column or box.

Figure 5-6 below is a check sheet being used to track five separate problems or symptoms simultaneously. In the far right-hand column, we are also evaluating the trend for each of these

Problem	Mon	Tues	Wed	Thur	Fri	Trend
Weight out of spec	ЖН	I I	I			→
Width out of spec	ЖН I I I	I I I I	I I			↘
Hole diameter too large	ЖН	ЖН	ЖН I I ЖН ЖН	ЖН ЖН ЖН ЖН	ЖН ЖН ЖН ЖН ЖН	↗
Hole diameter too small		ЖН		ЖН		∿∿∿
Hole out of position	ЖН	ЖН	ЖН	ЖН	ЖН	→

Figure 5-6.

81

problems or symptoms. Arrows can be used to symbolize what the product is doing as a function of time. In our example, weight and width problems appear to be diminishing, hole diameter (too large) is increasing, hole diameter (too small) is intermittent, and hole out of position is constant.

There are several steps to consider before you construct and use a check sheet of this nature:

1. Be certain that you completely define what you are looking for before you begin collecting information. That is, specifically define what the problem, symptom, defect, etc., is, so everyone involved in the data collection effort is looking for the same thing. If a measurement device will be used, make sure everyone who will use it knows how to use it and will use it the same way (e.g., perform a GR & R study if necessary). A good idea is to have a meeting with all concerned to explain fully what data are needed, when needed, why needed, how to collect the data and then answer any specific questions from the group related to the data collection exercise. Make sure that everyone involved understands the importance of accurate, consistent, and honest information.

2. Decide ahead of time when the data collection exercise begins and ends. That is, specifically what time does it start on what date and what time does it stop on what date.

3. If you are looking for a specific defect, decide upon the sampling plan, that is the number of samples to collect, the timing of sampling, etc.

4. Design a check sheet that is simple and easy to understand with all of the columns labeled clearly and correctly. Make sure you have enough space to collect the information you need.

Another type of useful check sheet is the picture sheet. The picture sheet is a sketch of the object with the defect and is used to identify defect frequency and location simultaneously. One simply places a tickmark on the picture sheet at the exact location of the defect and then observes any repeating patterns. If, for example, you were inspecting for blisters on a painted part, such as the hood of a car, or holes in rubber gloves, you would sketch the actual hood or glove as in Figure 5-7.

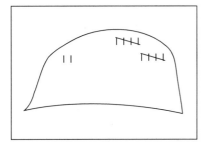 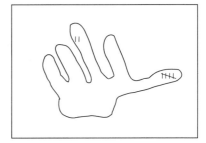

Figure 5-7.

By placing these tick marks directly on the sketches, it is easy to see if repeating patterns form that could provide direction for the problem-solving team. As I have demonstrated above, you don't have to be a great artist to use check sheets, and they are usually quite effective. If you're not an artist, then ask your engineering department to plot a miniature drawing of the part with the problem and use it as a check sheet.

Problem-Solving Truth #33: *Everyone has opinions about the cause of pro-blems, but opinions aren't facts and facts and data are what ultimately lead to the root cause of problems.*

5.4 SCATTERGRAMS

Sometimes during problem-solving exercises the team might be interested in determining whether two variables are interrelated. Is there a C&E relationship? One simple tool that can be used is a scattergram (or scatter diagram). The scattergram doesn't prove that one variable

Scattergrams

Two Variables
C & E Relationships
Strengths
X-Y Pairs
Line of Best Fit

causes the other, but it will tell you two very important things:

1. It demonstrates graphically whether the relationship exists.
2. It demonstrates if the relationship is strong or weak.

The scattergram is used to determine if two variables are related (i.e., is there a correlation?). The scattergram is set up by plotting data values of one variable (Variable 1) against data values of another (Variable 2). One variable represents the x-axis of an x-y graph and the other represents the y-axis. The points are plotted for a scattered pattern. If the two variables are related, then the points will be tightly packed and form a specific pattern. The strength of the relationship is directly proportional to the degree of scattering. That is, if there is very little scatter over the range of points tested, then the strength of the relationship is strong. Conversely, if the amount of scatter is great, then the relationship is weak. Figure 5-8 is an example of a scattergram.

Deciding whether a relationship or correlation exists between two variables and its strength is dependent upon the distinctiveness of the pattern formed and how tightly the points are packed together. In the above example, using these two criteria, we would conclude that there is a relationship and it appears to be strong.

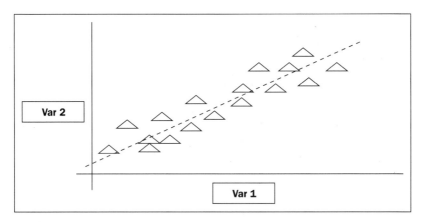

Figure 5-8.

Let's talk about a simple procedure for constructing a scat-tergram and then look at a real example.

1. Decide upon the C&E relationship that you wish to study (i.e., which two variables you believe might be related). Suppose we were interested in determining the relationship between molding pressure and part thickness.

2. Set Variable 1 (the cause) to a specific level and measure Variable 2's response (the effect). In our example, we would set our press to a specific pressure value, make a part, and then measure the part thickness. Again, select a different value for Variable 1, make a part, and measure Variable 2. Continue this process until you have studied a wide range of values that covers the normal operating range of the process range being studied. Since we're only trying to determine if a relationship exists and its relative strength, this procedure should only require, as a minimum, 20 x-y pairs or data points.

3. Draw a horizontal and a vertical line so that the bottom of the vertical and the left edge of the horizontal line

meet. This point is the zero point for both the x-axis (horizontal or cause) and y-axis (vertical or effect). Label the x and y axes with a sufficient data range so that the entire range of data points (i.e. x-y pairs) can be plotted. Also, place the name of the variable that's being investigated as the possible cause of the problem on the x-axis and the effect variable on the y-axis.

4. Plot each data point (i.e., measured values for x and y) on the scattergram at the appropriate x and y location.

5. Draw a line of best fit through the center of the data points, attempting to place an equal number of points on either side of the line.

Staying with our pressure/thickness example, suppose we followed steps 1 and 2 and collected the following data:

X (p.s.i.)	Y (mm)
100	2.0
200	4.2
300	11.7
400	16.1
500	21.0
600	24.1
700	28.3
800	32.5
900	36.4
1000	42.2

The scattergram of these x-y pairs is seen below in Figure 5-9.

On the x-axis, we have listed the press pressure range from 0 to 1000 p.s.i.; on the y-axis, the thickness range is 0 to 45 mm. These ranges cover the entire range of the data collected during the study of pressure versus thickness. We have also included the line of best fit we discussed in Step 5.

PRESSURE vs. THICKNESS

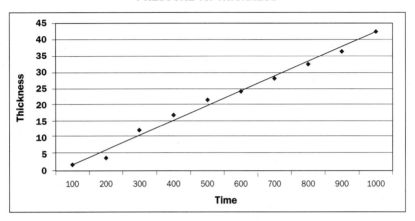

Figure 5-9.

Just exactly what did we learn from the plot of these two variables? Because the data points "hug" the line of best fit, we have discovered that the two variables are dependent upon each other. That is, as the pressure is changed from one value to another, the corresponding value for the thickness changes somewhat predictably. This predictability is positive. Therefore, as we increase the pressure upward, the thickness increases. In statistical terms we have determined that pressure and thickness correlate positively. This simply means that there is a strong C&E relationship and as x increases, y increases in a positive fashion.

On the other hand, if we increased the pressure and the thickness decreased we would conclude that there was a negative correlation. If the line of best fit curved in an upward fashion, then we would conclude that we had a curvilinear relationship. Finally, if the points did not hug the line of best fit, then the relationship is either weak or no relationship exists at all. In Figure 5-10, we see a variety of different relationships that could exist between two variables. Some are strong, some are weak, some are positive, some are negative, and still others are curvilinear. Let's explore each in a bit more detail.

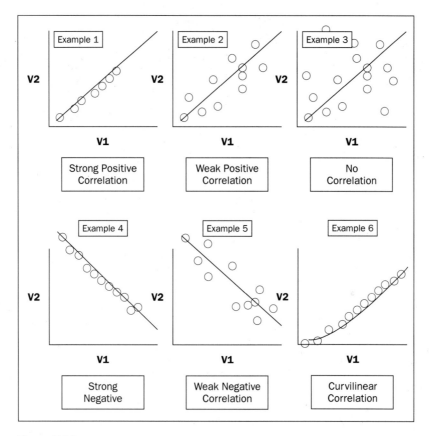

Figure 5-10.

In Example 1, we see a predictable relationship. As we increase the value of Variable 1 (V1), we see a predictable increase in Variable 2 (V2). In Example 2, we see the same C&E relationship, but our ability to predict V2 accurately as we change V1 is much less. In Example 3, no relationship exists between the two variables, so predicting V2 is not possible. In Example 4, we see a strong relationship, but this time as we increase V1, V2 decreases. In Example 5, we see the same C&E relationship as in Example 4, but again our ability to predict V2 is weak. In Example 6, we see a strong, non-linear relationship between V1 and V2. The scattergram is a simple and powerful tool that can be used to understand the process better by establishing C&E relationships, finding the root cause(s) of the problem, and ultimately correcting the problem.

Note: A blank scattergram is available in Appendix C for the reader to use and copy.

5.5 PROBLEM ASSIGNMENT

As soon as possible, after completion of this chapter, complete the following assignment:

Problem Assignment
Flow Chart
Run Chart
Check Sheet
Scattergram

1. Per the instructions in Section 5.1, construct (draw) a flow chart of the process with the problem defined in the assignment in Section 1.9.

2. Per the instructions in Section 5.2, collect data and construct (draw) a run chart. What is the trend of the data?

3. Per the instructions in Section 5.3, construct (draw) a check sheet for the process with the problem defined in the assignment in Section 1.9. and collect relevant information/data. Show the trend of the problem.

4. Per the instructions in Section 5.4, collect x-y pair data on two variables that you think might be related. Construct (draw) a scattergram using the data and draw a line of best fit. State (write) whether you believe there is or is not a C&E relationship and whether it is strong or weak and positive or negative. Explain (write) your answer.

What did you learn?

(In your own words, write the things you learned in this chapter and then compare them with what you should have learned.)

_____

_____

_____

_____

_____

_____

_____

_____

_____

_____

_____

_____

_____

CHAPTER 6

The Problem Analysis
Flow (PAF) Chart

What You Should Learn in This Chapter

What a Problem Analysis Flow (PAF) Chart is and
how to use it to get to the root cause of the problem.
Understand the sequence of steps in solving a problem.
How to develop an effective problem statement.
How to develop your approach to detecting
symptoms. What changes are important and
how to discover them.

In Chapter 1, we discussed the advantages of using a structured and systematic approach to problem solving. We also understood that any approach we use must be based upon basic reasoning, logic, and test data. We also learned about the importance of developing a complete definition of the problem and recording things like symptoms and known changes to the process. Next, we learned that to find defect-free configurations (DFCs) is important. Then, we looked for unique, different, or special distinctions about where (or when or how many) we have a problem compared to where we don't. In Chapter 4, we learned how to use valuable tools like why?-why? diagrams and causal chains.

In this chapter, we will examine a new tool that combines all of these individual elements from previous chapters into a single, usable format for solving problems. This tool, the Problem Analysis Flow (PAF) chart, combines all that we have learned into a single sheet and forces a logical, structured approach to solving problems.

The PAF chart contains ten major sections beginning with the development of a complete problem statement and ending with most probable cause(s) and short and long-term corrections. The ten sections of the PAF chart are the following:

1. The Problem Statement
2. Symptoms
3. Relevant Data
4. Changes
5. Defect-Free Configurations
6. Distinctions
7. Causal Chains II
8. Tests, Corrections, Results, and Conclusions
9. Most Probable Cause
10. Short-Term and Long-Term Corrections
    and Controls

Figure 6-1 is the front side of the PAF chart, containing the first eight sections. It is important to remember that each of the boxes on the front side of the PAF chart are numbered sequentially for a reason. That is, the number represents the order in which the box should be filled in. The Problem Statement is done first, followed by Symptoms, and so on. Don't skip around aimlessly.

Figure 6-2 is the reverse side of the PAF chart, containing the final two sections. The back side of the PAF chart is intended to provide additional space for recording overflow information from boxes 1-7 on the front side, the most probable cause(s) in box 9 and corrections and controls applied to the process in box 10. On a single sheet we have collected all of the information needed to correct the problem. What could be simpler than that!

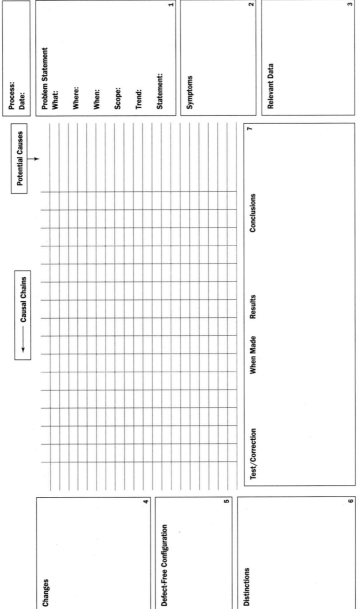

Figure 6-1.

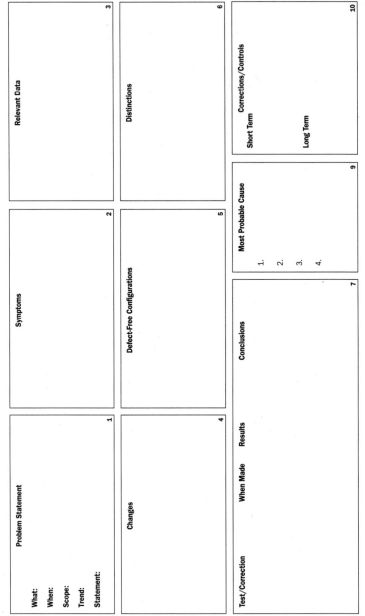

PROBLEM ANALYSIS FLOW CHART

Problem Statement — 1

What:
When:
Scope:
Trend:
Statement:

Symptoms — 2

Relevant Data — 3

Changes — 4

Defect-Free Configurations — 5

Distinctions — 6

Test/Correction   When Made   Results   Conclusions — 7

Most Probable Cause — 9

1.
2.
3.
4.

Corrections/Controls — 10

Short Term

Long Term

Figure 6-2.

6.1 THE PROBLEM STATEMENT

In developing the problem statement, we must view the problem from two different perspectives: the object and the defect or fault. The object is the process, machine, part, system, etc., that has had a change in performance. The defect is the

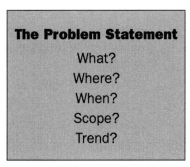

performance problem or what is perceived to be wrong with the object. When developing the problem statement, this concept of object and defect or fault must always be considered. Let's now look at the specific requirements for an effective problem statement.

PROBLEM STATEMENT
What: flow charts
Where: flow chart, check sheet
When: run chart, check sheet
Scope: check sheet
Trend: run chart, check sheet
Statement:

Figure 6-3.

Figure 6-3 "blown-up" version of the problem statement box from the PAF chart shown above. The basic components of this box are a series of questions relative to the "object" and the "defect" just presented. The questions should be answered as follows:

1. *What?* What is the specific object with the performance problem and what specifically on the

object is considered to be the fault, defect or performance problem? As indicated in the Figure 6-3, the team should develop a *flow chart* of the process to better understand and define the process with the defect or fault.

2. *Where?* Where is the object with the problem located and where physically on the object is the defect located? The team should construct and utilize a *flow chart* and *pictorial check sheet* to better understand the process and further define the location of the defect or fault.

3. *When?* When is the performance problem observed? That is, when, from a time perspective and when in the life cycle of the object or process or system, etc., is the fault seen? The team should construct a *run chart and a check sheet* to understand when the problem and symptoms of the problem started.

4. *Scope?* What is the scope of the performance problem? That is, how many objects have the defect and how much of the object is consumed with the defect? The team should construct and utilize a *run chart and check sheet* to understand the extent to which the problem has spread within the process.

5. *Trend?* What is the current rate of the performance problem and is the problem spreading to the remaining parts of the object? Is the performance problem increasing, decreasing, or remaining constant? The team should utilize a *run chart and check sheet* to better understand the current state of the problem. That is, is it increasing, decreasing, or remaining constant?

All five of these questions force the problem-solving team to assemble all the information needed to develop a complete definition of the problem at hand. How well the team does in assembling this information and how well they answer these questions sets the stage for the development of a complete problem statement. Because of this, care must be taken when answering these questions to assure that all of the information is accurate. Let's look at an example.

A problem-solving team is investigating the sudden stoppage of a punch press used to stamp metal parts. They investigate the problem and then answer the questions in the problem statement box as follows:

Problem Statement
What: J340 punch press
Piston #3
Where: On press line D
At the base of the piston
When: At 2:30 P.M., Tuesday, May 14, 1993
At step #4
After two months of operation
Scope: Only J340D punch press
Only on line D
Only on piston #3
Trend: Remaining constant
Statement: The piston on the J340D punch press on line D stopped working at 2:30 P.M. on Tuesday May 14, 1993, after two months of operation. No other presses have the problem.

Figure 6-4.

The team investigated the problem and found that a J340D punch press on line D suddenly stopped functioning. After observing the problem (i.e. taking the press apart) it appeared that the base of piston # 3 was defective for some reason. Based upon downtime records and conversations with the operator, the problem started at 2:30 P.M., Tuesday, May 14, 1993, after the press had been in operation for two months. The team also investigated the scope of the problem and found that only the J340D punch press on D line and only piston #3 was involved. This is an important fact because it more or less rules out a systemic problem (e.g., compressor malfunction). The team also concluded that the problem was isolated to the single press on D line.

Using all of this information the team was able to develop a comprehensive statement of the problem (see Figure 6-4) and in so doing were able to focus their efforts on the press with the performance problem.

Problem-Solving Truth #34: *When developing a problem statement, view the problem from two different perspectives: the object and the object's defect or fault.*

6.2 SYMPTOMS

How is it that we know when we have a problem? What signals us there has been a change in performance? Accompanying every problem are signs or indications that things aren't as they should be. It may be something as simple as the smell

Symptoms

Faults
Signs of Problems
Simultaneous
Senses

of burning rubber or the sound of bearings about to go. The sometimes-subtle signs are referred to as symptoms. Everyone at one time or another has been asked to describe the symptoms of something. The sick child, for example, may have an upset stomach or a fever, or clothes are not completely dry when removed from a clothes dryer. Both are common symptoms of a problem.

Symptoms are actually the faults that we observe. They are the deviations from the expected level of performance. Symptoms can range from obvious things like a machine making excessive noise to something as subliminal as a peculiar odor or minor tremors or vibrations. Some symptoms are easy to detect while others require more investigative rigor. Sometimes, multiple symptoms occur at the same time (simultaneous symptoms). Usually simultaneous symptoms come from a common cause.

When describing symptoms it is important to be as descriptive and detailed as possible. When we develop causal chains in box 7 of the PAF chart (see Figure 6-1), we will refer to and utilize the symptoms. What is the best way to recognize symptoms? The old expression that we learned in our grade school days (at least us old timers), "Stop! Look! and Listen!" before crossing the street is a good place to start. This expression implies that we should use our seeing and hearing senses before proceeding further. When we are developing our list of symptoms, we should do the same.

Consider the first thing your doctor does prior to making his diagnosis. Your doctor checks your eyes, ears, nose and throat (looks and listens). He or she checks your heart beat (listens), checks your pulse (feels and listens), and checks your abdomen (feels). Just like your doctor, you should use all of your senses when investigating a problem and creating a list of symptoms.

SYMPTOMS
1. What was heard?
2. What was seen?
3. What was smelled?
4. What was felt?

Figure 6-5.

Figure 6-5 is a miniature version of the box in the PAF chart and contains four questions that should be asked when developing your list of symptoms. Try asking the following questions when you're developing a list of symptoms:

- "What was heard when the defect or fault occurred?'
- "What was seen when the defect or fault occurred?"
- "What was smelled when the defect or fault occurred?"
- "What was felt when the defect or fault occurred?"

SYMPTOMS
1. Loud, grinding, scraping noise, like metal on metal.
2. Strong odor, like burning electrical wires.
3. Piston # 3 won't retract.
4. Motor stopped running.
5. Press stopped.

Figure 6-6.

Let's go back to our example and see what our problem-solving team discovered when searching for symptoms (see Figure 6-6). The operator who was running the punch press described the symptoms that he heard as a loud, grinding, scraping noise, like metal on metal. He also smelled a strong odor that he described as "like burning electrical wires." The team investigated and saw that piston #3 would not retract. The operator also stated that the press stopped because the motor stopped running.

In addition to these questions, other important bits of information should be recorded as well: the overall cleanliness and orderliness of the area, any equipment leaks like oil, water, coolant, etc. These observations could very well be important information to the team. The team must use all their powers of observation in the hunt for symptoms and then develop a complete and accurate description of all of the symptoms.

Problem-Solving Truth #35: *Symptoms are the faults we observe, so use your senses to develop the symptoms.*

6.3 RELEVANT DATA

In your experiences in problem solving, how many times have you gotten deep into the process only to find that you were missing some key information and you had to go search for it. In this section, we will look for

Relevant Data

Who Was Involved?
Other Witnesses?
What Was Being Used?
Environmental Conditions?

things that could be relevant later to help resolve confusing or puzzling points. Much like the problem statement and symptoms sections, the team might ask some key questions to develop the relevant data box.

RELEVANT DATA
1. Who was involved and who might have witnessed?
2. What was being used and What were the environmental conditions?

Figure 6-7.

Figure 6-7 is a miniature version of the relevant data box in the PAF chart. It contains two basic questions that should be asked when developing this section: Who and What. Let's explore these two questions in a bit more detail.

1. Who was involved in the process when the first symptoms appeared? If a piece of equipment was involved, who was the operator or operators running it when the symptoms first appeared?
2. What specifically was being used on the process when the symptoms first became visible? Again, if we're talking about a machine that produces a part or product, then what were the specific materials being used? This would include lot numbers, serial numbers, a description of the materials, etc. Be specific!

3. Who else might have witnessed the onset of the first symptoms? Was a material handler at the machine? How about an inspector or supervisor? How about another machine operator nearby? Anyone involved might have the missing piece in this puzzle, and your job is to find it.

4. What were the environmental conditions in the area where the problem occurred? Was it hot or cold, and if so, what was the temperature? Was it humid or dry, and if so, what was the humidity? Was it a dusty environment? Did any unusual things like oil, water, or coolant leaks occur? Did the equipment look worn? What about process gage readings? Were they all reading where they should be?

Let's look at our punch press example and see what this team recorded.

In our example (see Figure 6-8), the relevant data included in box #3 was a listing of the machine operator, John Jones and the material handler, Janet Thompkins. Both should be considered as team members because both have valuable information that will help find the root cause of the problem with the punch press. This is especially true of John Jones, the machine operator.

The team also found that the hardened steel being run on this press was also being run on two other presses and neither of

RELEVANT DATA
1. John Jones was running the press when the symptoms first appeared.
2. Hardened steel – lot #00012-AB was being run when the symptoms first appeared. The same lot # was running on press JD5-01 on line C and JD5-09 on line A.
3. Janet Thompkins, material handler, also observed the first symptoms.
4. The shop temperature was 89°F and the % RH was 68.

Figure 6-8.

these presses had experienced the stoppage problem. This would appear to eliminate the material as a suspect.

The team also found a temperature and humidity device and found the shop temperature to be 89°F and the relative humidity to be 68 percent. This information may or may not be relevant, but it's available in case it is.

6.4 CHANGES

Problems never occur without reasons. Problems *always follow changes*. The change or changes might have occurred immediately prior to the onset of the problem or long before and is just now manifesting itself. The change may even be repetitive and could be confused with an intermittent problem.

Changes
Documentation
Open-ended Questions
Process Check
Process Changes
Material Changes
People Changes

Finding the change or changes is absolutely paramount to solving the problem. In fact, if you don't find the change, you won't solve the problem. You may hide it with band-aid fixes, but you won't solve it. If you don't solve it, I promise you it will return!

The most effective way to find changes is by searching through documentation and—you guessed it—by asking questions. Let's talk about asking questions for a minute. Remember several basic things when interviewing people who might have knowledge of the process with the problem. First, always use *open-ended questions*. That is, use questions that require more than a yes or no answer. For example, instead of asking "Did you hear anything out of the ordinary when the symptoms first appeared?," ask "What did you hear when the symptoms first appeared?" Allow the person to reach into his or her memory banks and reconstruct the sequence of events in his or her own words. Second, *ask follow-up questions* to define further exactly what happened. For example, suppose the operator says, "I heard a grinding, scraping noise." Your follow-up question might be, "Do you mean like metal on metal?" Finally, when you've completed the interview, do a *process check* by summarizing and stating what you think you heard.

CHANGES
1. Process settings?
2. Modifications or improvements?
3. Major/minor maintenance?
4. Preventive maintenance?
5. Raw materials?
6. Environmental conditions?
7. Shutdowns or start-ups?
8. Operators?
9. Speeds or production rates?
10. Utilities?

Figure 6-9.

Figure 6-9 is a miniature version of the one in the PAF chart that contains a list of potential changes to the process that the team should investigate and document. Let's explore each of these in a bit more detail.

1. *Adjustments to process settings.* These are sometimes the most difficult to find because not all changes are documented. Sometimes, well-intentioned (but not trained) operators, supervisors, engineers, managers tweak the equipment and don't tell anyone or document what they did. This special category of change (variation) sometimes is referred to as tampering. By the way, I don't care how good your facility is and how much control you think you have over change, tampering goes on in your facility!

2. *Modifications or improvements to the process.* These types of changes include well-studied and unstudied, well-documented and undocumented, well-planned and unplanned improvements that may have an impact on how equipment or processes run after they are implemented. These may very well have been solutions to past problems. Remember what we said earlier: "Today's problems are sometimes yesterday's solutions." So, be careful.

3. *Major or minor maintenance work on a process.* This category of change includes simple tightening of nuts and belts to major overhauls. It includes both simple and complex work done by maintenance and is sometimes not documented. It has been my experience that no matter what is written on the work order, maintenance always finds something else that needs an adjustment and since they are already on the equipment, they might as well "fix that, too!"

4. *Preventive maintenance (PM) activities.* PM is by far one of the most important activities in every manu-facturing facility. If done correctly, it is specific in nature and usually requires little effort in the search for documentation. But we all know that other things get done as part of the PM activities that never get documented.

5. *Changes to raw materials.* This is sometimes an elusive change because process changes at the supplier's location are rarely communicated to the customer. I'm not talking about formulation changes, but rather those same changes that you make in your own process in the name of tweaking the process. Although we would like to believe that our supplier base would never do anything to change the product characteristics, it has the same control problems that

you do. If you don't believe that, then you better get a reality check!

6. *Changes to environmental conditions.* Although we would like to believe that the products we are producing are robust over a wide range of temperature and humidity ranges, they probably aren't. If you are fortunate enough to produce a product in an environmentally controlled facility, then you may have never experienced the impact of outside air on inside air and ultimately the product and process. Conditions can include dust levels, sand (if you have to sand your products) and paint particles (if you have to paint the product, too).

7. *Shutdowns and startups.* Shutdowns and restarts create a real dilemma for the problem-solving team because, again, they aren't always documented. We all know that a product at the beginning of the run is not the same as the product at the middle or end of the run. If things like pressure and temperature stabilization are important factors in your process, then you know how important it is to know when these changes in run conditions occur.

8. *Changes in operators.* No two operator work methods are ever the same, especially if work methods are labor-intensive. Operators are usually looking for ways to do the job faster and more efficiently. This is perfectly acceptable if the method change is studied and documented. In the real world, however, this is not always the case! I know it's hard to believe, but some operators even know the correct method and purposely change it because "they know better than management!" Fortunately this is usually the exception rather than the rule.

9. *Changes in speeds or production rates.* Faster! Faster! Faster! More! More! More! This seems to be the norm in a manufacturing environment. This, too, is acceptable if it is done under control and is documented, which is not the case all of the time, however.

10. *Changes in utilities.* Sometimes, even in the best facilities, there are changes in things like air pressure, line voltage, etc., that remain undetected until these changes create a change in performance.

All of these changes must be investigated by the problem-solving team. Incidentally, if your company isn't currently documenting these changes, then it's probably a good idea to use this list of changes as a template for what should be documented. It is a good idea to have a process change log at each piece of time-based equipment. That is, have a place to record the change, the date and time of the change, who authorized the change, who made the change, etc. Remember, all problems are preceded by change of some kind, so by documenting the changes in detail, you will facilitate your problem-solving activities and potentially avoid problems altogether. Let's take a look at the changes our team was able to find.

CHANGES
1. New press operator due to illness.
2. Changed from Apco to Steelco (steel suppliers) on May 14, 1993.
3. PM done on punch press on May 13, 1993.
4. New maintenance mechanic hired April 12, 1993 (performed PM).
5. Piston #3 replaced as part of the PM on May 13, 1993.

Figure 6-10.

As you can see in Figure 6-10, the team was able to determine some potentially significant changes. It determined a new operator was on the press due to an illness. They also changed steel suppliers from Apco to Steelco at about the time the problem surfaced. There was also a PM done on the press in question and it was done by a newly hired maintenance mechanic. They were also able to determine that the piston in question, piston #3, was changed during the PM.

All of these changes were potentially the root cause of the problem with the press. Was the team able to determine all of the changes that occurred prior to the appearance of the first symptoms? I would say probably not, but because it was able to find changes, the team had a chance to find the root cause.

One final time, make sure that *all changes are documented!*

Problem-Solving Truth #36: *Problems never occur without reason; they always follow changes.*

6.5 DEFECT-FREE CONFIGURATIONS

When individual parts are linked together for the purpose of performing a distinct function, this linkage is referred to as a configuration. An automobile, for example, has numerous examples of configurations. The transmission is one example where components (e.g.,

> **DFCs**
> Configurations
> Defect Free
> Still Functioning
> Components

shafts, cams, pinions, clutches) are linked together to allow the car to move backward and forward at different speeds. When the car is in drive, we know that the car should move forward and when it's in reverse it should move backward. Many of the components that work to move the car forward also work to make the car go backward. They are, however, considered separate configurations.

Suppose a problem develops with the transmission and your car will now only move backward. Here we would say that reverse configuration is considered to be a defect-free configuration (DFC). Since the forward configuration is no longer functioning, it is not. Though the total configuration isn't functioning normally, the components of the forward configurations that are still functioning normally are considered to be DFCs. We, therefore, define a DFC as "the combination of components in a nonfunctioning or functioning system that are functioning normally." So, why should you care about DFCs?

Identifying DFCs is important because they help us eliminate potential problem causes, since the components of a DFC are still functioning and help us point out differences or distinctions.

DEFECT-FREE CONFIGURATIONS
1. What is still functioning in:
a. The non-functioning process, system or equipment?
b. Other identical or like processes, systems or equipment?

Figure 6-11.

The box to the right Figure 6-11 is a miniature version of the one found in the PAF chart and it contains two basic areas of concentration the team should focus on when searching for DFCs. Let's explore these two areas in a bit more detail.

The fact that parts of the process, system, or equipment with the problem are still functioning is important as we trace the chain of events that led to the problem's origin. Knowing what is still functioning helps the team locate the problem-solving "black box." On the other hand, by observing other identical or like processes, systems, or equipment, we form a basis for comparison in the next step of the problem-solving process. Let's look at our example one more time (see Figure 6-12).

The team had to disassemble the press to view the individual configurations to determine what was still functioning and what wasn't. By doing so, they were able to find out that the clutch, crank, and flywheel assembly were still functioning. The team

DEFECT-FREE CONFIGURATIONS
1. Clutch, crank and flywheel assembly.
2. Punch and die assembly.
3. Pistons 1, 2, and 4.
4. Other identical presses.

Figure 6-12.

also identified the punch and die assembly and pistons 1, 2, and 4 as being DFCs as well. Finally, since the problem did not exist on the other identical presses, they, too, were considered DFCs.

Problem-Solving Truth #37: *Identifying defect-free configurations (DFCs) is important because DFCs help us eliminate potential causes of problems.*

6.6 DISTINCTIONS

Let's return to our car for a moment that only moves in reverse. If we were trying to understand the reason why it only moves backward, we might start with a basic question like, "What is different or unique or special about why it won't go forward compared to why it will go

Distinctions
Unique?
Special?
Different?
Comparison
Broken vs. Working

backward?" If we can answer this basic question, then chances are we will be able to pinpoint the most probable cause of the problem. This difference between where we have the problem and where we don't is referred to as a distinction.

A distinction is always the result of a comparison between what is no longer functioning and what is still functioning, or what is broken and what is working, rather than comparing what works to what doesn't. The focus of our attention should always be directed toward what isn't functioning properly.

DISTINCTIONS
What is unique, special or different about:
1. What is defective versus what is not?
2. Where we have the problem versus where we don't?
3. When we have the problem versus when we don't?

Figure 6-13.

Figure 6-13 is a miniature version of the one in the PAF chart. Inside, three basic questions will help us zero in on the distinctions. Let's look at these questions in a bit more detail.

1. What is unique, special, or different between what is not functioning (or is defective) and what is functioning (or is not defective)?
2. What is unique, special, or different between where we have the problem (or defect) compared to where we don't?
3. What is unique, special, or different about when we have the problem (or defect) compared to when we don't?

In order to uncover distinctions, we are interested in finding out the What, the Where, and the When of the differences.

Let's, once again, look at what the team came up with concerning distinctions.

In Figure 6-14, four distinctions were identified: a new piston on the press with the problem; a new mechanic, as part of his training, assigned only to the press with the problem; only the press with the problem had a PM, and the mounting bolts on piston #3 were loose compared to the bolts on pistons 1, 2, and 4.

Remember, when looking for distinctions, always compare the object or system or process with the problem to the object or system or process without the problem. Distinctions are just another piece to the problem-solving puzzle.

DISTINCTIONS
1. New piston #3 on press with problem.
2. New mechanic assigned to only the press with the problem.
3. PM only done on press with the problem.
4. Mounting bolts on piston #3 are loose compared to bolts on pistons 1, 2, and 4.

Figure 6-14.

Problem-Solving Truth #38: *Always compare the process or object with the problem to the process or object without the problem, not vice versa. It's easier to see distinctions.*

6.7 CAUSAL CHAINS II

In Section 4.4, I introduced you to a problem-solving tool called causal chains. Causal chains are the centerpiece of the PAF chart and provide an effective means for determining the root cause of problems. They are simple to use and compel the team to take an in-depth look at the process with the problem.

Causal Chains

Logical Steps
Symptoms to Root
Causes
Ask Why?
Chain of Events

Causal chains are logical steps from the symptoms to the cause of the problem. Each step is the cause of the next step and the effect of the previous one. The information on the step to the left is always the cause of the information on the step to the right.

Let's look at the punch press problem and see how the team developed their causal chain. Remember the problem? The J340D punch press on line D stopped working at 2:30 P.M., Tuesday May 14, 1993, after two months of operation. As our causal chain develops, utilize all of the other information available from the symptoms, relevant data, changes, DFCs, and

112

distinction boxes to help form the chain of events that led to the change in performance.

When creating causal chains, always start with the symptoms of the problem. Start by asking, "Are any of the symptoms simultaneous or is one the cause of another?" If they aren't simultaneous, then they are independent and will either fall in separate causal chains or separate links of one chain. On the PAF chart, list the symptoms from box 2 in the potential cause column.

In the example, the team identified four symptoms. Upon discussing these symptoms with John Jones, the machine operator, and Janet Thompkins, the material handler, both heard the loud, grinding, scraping noise followed by the piston stopping followed by the odor of burning electrical wiring followed by the motor stopping and finally the press stopping. Since the press stopping was the last symptom, the team started with it by placing the object (press) on top of the step and its state (stopped) directly beneath it. In our example, all of the symptoms were independent and one was the cause of the next. The next step in constructing the causal chain is considering or hypothesizing potential causes. Only causes that could explain or account for the symptoms should be considered. Always develop the causal chain based upon facts, relevant data, changes, and distinctions listed in boxes 3, 4, and 6 respectively.

Use the DFCs in box 5 to eliminate possible causes. For example, since the same steel was being used on other presses, the team felt that it could eliminate the steel as a cause.

In Figure 6-15, the team created only one causal chain. It begins with the press stopping and continues from right to left by asking the question Why.

The press stopped because the motor stopped. Why did the motor stop? The motor stopped because the armature burned out—perhaps burning electrical wiring? Why did the armature burn out? The team hypothesized that this could occur if either the armature was defective or it was in an over-current condition. After checking the armature and finding it not defective, the team literally "crossed it out" as a potential cause.

The team continued the development of the causal chain by returning to the armature over-current step questioning why it was over-current. They hypothesized that this could occur if either the motor was in an overload condition or the circuit breaker had failed and tested the circuit breaker to find that it was indeed, defective. The team could have jumped to the conclusion that the root cause of the press stopping was a defective circuit breaker, but they might have been wrong because they still hadn't determined why the motor was in overload.

The team asked the question, "Why was the motor in an overload condition?" and concluded that either the material could have been too hard or that the material (steel) had jammed. They eliminated the material hardness question because the same steel was being used on other presses without a problem.

Then the team asked the question, "What would have caused the material to jam?" Again, after discussion, they developed three possibilities:

1. The piston could have been defective.
2. The piston was loose.
3. The operator had made a mistake while loading the material.

Each possibility was considered; since the piston had been working well all day, it probably wasn't defective and the team eliminated the piston. A lead hand had been running the press; after discussing this possibility with him, the team also ruled his effect out. That left the piston loose as the remaining potential cause of the jam.

Again, the team asked, "What would cause the piston to be loose?" Four bolts secure the piston, so if the piston was loose, then a good possibility existed that the bolts were loose. The team returned to the relevant data box and found that it hadn't

THE PROBLEM ANALYSIS FLOW CHART

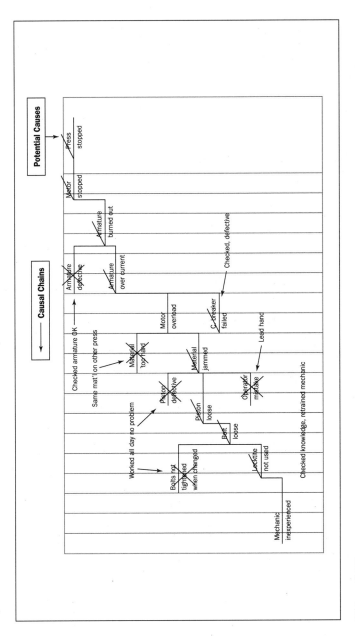

Figure 6-15.

115

determined the name of the "new maintenance mechanic" so they could ask him questions about his PM work. The team went to maintenance, got his name, found him, and asked him to describe how he had changed piston #3. He told the team that he had simply tightened the bolts with a wrench. When the team asked if he had used Locktite as part of the change procedure, he told them he had not. Voila! The team had discovered the root cause to be an inexperienced mechanic not knowing that he should have used Locktite to secure the bolts. The team had systematically, using a very structured approach, discovered the root cause. By so doing, they were able to account for all of the symptoms.

Note how the team systematically stepped through the problem and eliminated some of the possible causes as they went. When they eliminated potential causes, the team simply "X'd" the cause out and moved on.

One other point on causal chains is the use of diagonal lines on the steps. In Section 4.4, we said that the addition of a diagonal line at the elbow of the step indicates that the object is in an abnormal state. In the case of the motor being overloaded, this would normally be considered an abnormal state. Since the circuit breaker was found to be faulty, then the motor overload was considered a normal state.

In Summary

- Use the symptoms box to begin your causal chain and discuss whether the symptoms are independent or not.
  - Use the relevant data, DFCs, and distinctions boxes to eliminate potential causes.
  - Consider changes and distinctions that could link to a cause. A distinction sometimes helps you identify a change that, in turn, may explain a symptom.
  - If more than one causal chain exists, look for causes that could be common to both of them.
  - Always make sure you have accounted for or explained all of the symptoms.

In our example, the team explained the noise (caused by a jam that sheared the steel), the odor (burned out armature), the piston not retracting (because of the jam it was wedged), the motor stopping (no current), and finally the press stopping (the motor had stopped). If the team hadn't explained or accounted for all of the symptoms, then they would have had to carry out some checks or tests.

In the example, the motor should not have overloaded because the circuit breaker should have tripped. Tests and checks were conducted on the circuit breaker and determined that the circuit breaker was faulty. In Section 6.8, we enter this check along with the results. As a side note, this circuit breaker problem should have been identified during the PM since this was one of the PM checklist items. This was an independent cause that contributed to the press failure.

The causal chain forces us to look at the entire system of causes and not just the symptoms. In many cases, the circuit breaker problem might not have been identified and corrected, thus creating a new problem in the future.

6.8 TESTS, CORRECTIONS, RESULTS, AND CONCLUSIONS

As the team stepped through the chain of events via the causal chains, tests and results, observations, corrections, and conclusions were made along the way. The PAF chart has a special place for this

Tests, Corrections, Results & Conclusions

Tests Run
Corrections Made
Results of Tests
Observations
Conclusions Developed

information, box 8, where we list all tests, corrections, results, and conclusions.

Why did we create this box? Each time a problem-solving team steps through a problem, it should become a case study for future reference. Think about it: if a team has gone to all the trouble of solving a problem, isn't it possible that the same or similar problem could occur elsewhere? If we translate our findings to other situations we should limit repeating these steps, but in reality we don't always do this. The PAF charts become historical record and potential learning tools for the future. Figure 6-16 is a miniature version of the one in the PAF

TESTS, CORRECTIONS, RESULTS, AND CONCLUSIONS			
TESTS/CORRECTIONS	WHEN MADE	RESULTS	CONCLUSIONS
List all tests performed to validate or eliminate potential problem causes. List all corrections made to the process when obvious, correctable problems were discovered	List date and times that any tests were performed or changes were made.	List the results of any tests or effects corrections made to the process.	List any conclusions made by the team as a result of tests or corrections made.

Figure 6-16.

chart and contains a description of what should be included in this box. This box serves as a receptacle for all of the facts that the team used to logically solve the problem.

In Figure 6-17, we have listed all tests, corrections, results and conclusions. We have listed the check of the armature, circuit breaker, and piston as well as a check of training records on the mechanic involved in the problem.

As the team moved through the causal chain section of the PAF chart, it recorded other conclusions not requiring tests directly in the causal chain section of the PAF chart. For example, the team eliminated the material being too hard by drawing from the information contained in the relevant data box. The same can be said as to why they eliminated the operator mistake relative to the jammed steel. When the team discovered that the mechanic didn't know about using Locktite, they

TESTS, CORRECTIONS, RESULTS, AND CONCLUSIONS			
TESTS/CORRECTIONS	WHEN MADE	RESULTS	CONCLUSIONS
Check armature for functionality	May 14, 1993 @ 4:00PM	No apparent problems	Replace because of burnout
Check circuit breaker for functionality	May 14, 1993 @ 4:30 PM	Stuck, not functional, switch faulty	Replaced switch
Check defective piston #3	May 14, 1993	Functional	OK
Checked training records on mechanic	May 15, 1993	Locktite use not included in training materials	Mechanic didn't know about use of Locktite— update training plan

Figure 6-17.

simply re-instructed the mechanic on the spot and noted that in the causal chain section of the PAF chart. It also recorded significant data such as the results of the conversation with the inexperienced mechanic directly on the chart. My advice to you is record it wherever you feel most comfortable.

Problem-Solving Truth #39: *Whenever possible, test to eliminate potential root causes.*

6.9 MOST PROBABLE CAUSE

On the reverse side of the PAF chart is a place to record the Most Probable Cause. In this section, the team should review all of its analysis and after much discussion, list what it feels was the underlying

Most Probable Cause

Review Analysis

Discussion

Conclusions

Root Cause

cause for the problem (i.e., the root cause).

Figure 6-18 is a miniature version of the one in the PAF chart and contains a list of questions that should be asked to arrive at the most probable cause of the problem. There are three basic considerations when contemplating the root cause(s).

1. The elimination of potential root causes that didn't contribute to the problem.
2. The construction of the causal chain in such a fashion to have included all of the possible chains.
3. The inclusion of all possible tests to eliminate or validate potential root causes.

MOST PROBABLE CAUSE
1. Have I accounted for or eliminated the nonpotential root causes?
2. Did I carry the causal chain to its entire length, i.e., did I ask Why far enough and did I include all of the possible chains?
3. Based upon the flow of information in the causal chain and the results of testing, what is the most probable cause?

Figure 6-18.

In our example, what do you feel was the root cause? Was it the jammed steel? Was it the defective circuit breaker? Let's look at what our team concluded.

MOST PROBABLE CAUSE
1. Inexperienced mechanic.
2. Training records didn't include the use of Locktite.
3. Defective circuit breaker.
4. Mechanic certification process.
5. Mechanic didn't check circuit breaker during PM.

Figure 6-19.

The team reviewed all of the information contained in the PAF chart, but focused their collective energy on the causal chain. It asked specific questions like "Was the root cause of the problem an inexperienced mechanic?" and "Was it a problem with the training of new mechanics?" They also asked questions like "Did we perform all of the necessary tests to eliminate or validate the potential root causes?" and "Did we include all of the possible causal chains?" The root cause of any problem lies at the end of the causal chain, but the question is where do you stop with the causal chain? The team's final entry or step was an inexperienced mechanic.

The real question that must be answered is, "What must be corrected to avoid a repeat of the problem?" In the example, should we avoid using inexperienced mechanics from performing PMs? Or, should we take a look at how we certify new mechanics? We know that the training plan did not include the use of Locktite, so if we update the training to include this, will the problem disappear? Our team listed five most likely most probable causes and they were right. The fact is, a problem can have multiple root causes with each requiring a separate action. Some of the root causes directly contributed to the failure while others indirectly contributed. All require actions aimed at elimination of a repeat failure.

Problem-Solving Truth #40: *Problems may have multiple root causes with each producing separate symptoms and each requiring separate actions.*

6.10 SHORT-TERM AND LONG-TERM CORRECTIONS AND CONTROLS

What's the difference between short-term and long-term corrections? What about the difference between short-term and long-term and controls? Figure 6-20 summarizes these differences.

Corrections and Control

Short Term

Immediate

Long Term

Future

CORRECTIONS AND CONTROLS
Short Term
Corrections
1. *Short term*: Corrections implemented immediately to resolve the problem
2. *Long term*: Systemic or more complicated corrections to avoid future failures.
Controls
1. *Short term*: Checks put in place to detect defects or defaults.
2. *Long term*: Actions taken to prevent a repeat of the problem (e.g., Pokayokes).

Figure 6-20.

1. *Short-term corrections*: Those actions that can be implemented immediately to resolve the problem.
2. *Long-term corrections*: Those actions that are either systemic or more complicated to implement that will result in an avoidance of the failure in the future.
3. *Short-term controls*: Checks that detect the problem after it has occurred.
4. *Long-term controls*: Actions taken to prevent a repeat of the problem. The most common form of this is failsafe devices or Pokayokes.

In the example, several corrections and actions occurred immediately. These included things like replacing the defective circuit breaker and retraining the inexperienced mechanic. There were other items that required longer-term corrective actions like why the training records didn't list the use of Lock-tite or why the mechanic didn't check the circuit breaker. Both types of corrections require completely different actions.

With short-term actions, the problem is fixed on the spot. With long-term corrections, a complete review of the systems in place must be carried out to determine what systems failed or what systems need to be put in place to avoid a repeat failure. Figure 6-21 is what our team recommended. The team listed short-term corrective actions as the replacement of the defective circuit breaker, an update of the training materials to include the use of Locktite, and the retraining of the mechanic on the use of Locktite and the correct use of the PM checklist. They also updated the PM checklist and implemented an audit to assure PM checklist items were completed. All of these can be done immediately without much effort.

The long-term corrective actions require more effort. The team suggested a review of how training materials were approved for use. They also recommended a review of the cer-

---

CORRECTIONS AND CONTROLS

Short Term

Corrections

1. Replaced defective circuit breaker.
2. Update training materials to include the use of Locktite.
3. Retrain mechanic on use of Locktite and use of PM checklist.

Controls

1. Update PM checklist and implement an audit of PMs.

Long Term

Corrections

1. Review how training materials are approved.
2. Review maintenance certification process for new mechanics.

Control

1. Implement Pokayoke to assure bolts are tight.

Figure 6-21.

tification process used by maintenance for new mechanics. In place of a long-term control, the team recommended the implementation of a Pokayoke or failsafe device to assure that loose bolts are no longer an issue. Has it addressed all of the issues? Yes! Will the corrective actions work? We hope so!

6.11 PROBLEM ASSIGNMENT

As soon as possible, after completion of this chapter, using the PAF chart, complete the following assignment:

> **Assignment**
> New Problem
> Problem Statement
> PAF Chart
> Most Probable Cause
> Correction

1. Select a "new" problem (i.e., different than assignment 1.10) from the work place and create (write) a problem statement per the instructions in Sections 1.4 and 4.1.
2. Per the instructions in Section 4.2, investigate and list (write) the symptoms associated with the problem in 1 above.
3. Per the instructions in Section 4.3, investigate and list (write) any relevant data associated with the problem in 1 above.
4. Per the instructions in Section 4.4, investigate and list (write) any changes that occurred prior to the appearance of the first symptoms of the problem associated with 1 above.
5. Per the instructions listed in Section 4.5, investigate and list (write) any DFCs related to the problem identified in 1 above.

6. Per the instructions listed in Section 4.6, investigate and list (write) any distinctions related to the problem identified in 1 above.

7. Per the instructions listed in Section 4.7, construct (draw) a causal chain (s) related to the problem identified in 1 above.

8. In the instructions listed in Section 4.8, list (write) all tests, corrections, results and conclusions related to the problem identified in 1 above.

9. Per the instructions listed in Section 4.9, list (write) most probable causes related to the problem identified in 1. above.

10. Per the instructions in Section 4.10, list (write) the short- and long-term corrections and controls for the problem identified in 1 above.

What did you learn?

(In your own words, write the things you learned in this chapter and then compare them with what you should have learned.)

_____

_____

_____

_____

_____

_____

_____

_____

_____

_____

_____

_____

APPENDIX A

Problem-Solving Truths

Problem-Solving Truth #1: *All problems are the direct result of changes that occurred prior to the new level of performance.*

Problem-Solving Truth #2: *Deviations in performance don't become problems unless they have a negative impact on the organization, their root cause is unknown, or it costs too much or takes too much time to fix them.*

Problem-Solving Truth #3: *People will avoid problem-solving opportunities if they lack problem-solving skills, haven't successfully solved problems in the past, aren't appreciated when they do solve problems, or feel threatened by the situation.*

Problem-Solving Truth #4: *Systematic methods only appear to take longer than the "change something and see what happens" approach.*

Problem-Solving Truth #5: *Problem-solving success is not the result of superior knowledge.*

Problem-Solving Truth #6: *Structured approaches to solving problems will only be successful if they are established as the norm.*

Problem-Solving Truth #7: *Today's problem solutions could very well be tomorrow's problems if the right questions aren't asked.*

Problem-Solving Truth #8: *Generally speaking, today's problems are yesterday's solutions implemented without data.*

Problem-Solving Truth #9: *When describing a problem, always view the problem from two separate perspectives: the object and the object's defect or fault.*

Problem-Solving Truth #10: *Use all of your senses when searching for symptoms.*

Problem-Solving Truth #11*: Effective problem analysis attempts to relate the problem to symptoms, differences, changes, and times.*

Problem-Solving Truth #12: *It is important to understand that problems might have multiple root causes.*

Problem-Solving Truth #13: *Identifying potential problem causes is the result of a logical and systematic look at all available information. It is never the result of guessing.*

Problem-Solving Truth #14: *Don't ever be afraid to ask for help when solving problems. Asking for help is not a weakness; it is a sign of intelligence.*

Problem-Solving Truth #15: *Don't ever assume a problem has only one cause.*

Problem-Solving Truth #16: *The priority in problem solving is always stopping the negative effect of the problem first, then implementing true solutions and preventive actions.*

Problem-Solving Truth #17: *Never implement a solution and then assume it is failsafe. Always validate that your solution does not have a negative impact on the process in question. Always test the impact of your solution before you declare success.*

Problem-Solving Truth #18: *Never let any problem-solving tool completely replace your ability to reason and exercise good judgment.*

Problem-Solving Truth #19: *Symptoms are always a sign that something has changed or is wrong.*

Problem-Solving Truth #20: *Simultaneous symptoms usually have a common cause.*

Problem-Solving Truth #21: *Independent causes do not or may not occur simultaneously.*

Problem-Solving Truth #22: *Find defect-free configurations and then compare to find differences and distinctions.*

Problem-Solving Truth #23: *Problem-solving traps create detours for problem solvers. You can't eliminate them, but it helps to know they exist.*

Problem-Solving Truth #24: *Incorrect data are actually more dangerous than no data because they lead you down the wrong path.*

Problem-Solving Truth #25: *The key to finding the root cause of intermittent problems is determining the timing of symptoms and then relating them to changes.*

Problem-Solving Truth #26: *Recurring problems are always the direct result of inadequate or incomplete problem-solving techniques.*

Problem-Solving Truth #27: *Every problem is a treasure because it represents an opportunity for the organization to improve.*

Problem-Solving Truth #28: *Effective problem solving is the synergistic result of a functionally diverse team using a structured approach.*

Problem-Solving Truth #29: *Membership on a problem-solving team should be limited to people who have a vested interest in the process with the problem.*

Problem-Solving Truth #30: *When problems are discovered and investigated, a chain of events always lead to the problem source or root cause.*

Problem-Solving Truth #31: *Most processes are dynamic and changing so it is important to study them over time. This is especially true with labor-intensive processes.*

Problem-Solving Truth #32: *When plotting data using time as an x-axis, always put the data in production order before plotting.*

Problem-Solving Truth #33: *Everyone has opinions about the cause of problems, but opinions aren't facts and facts and data are what ultimately lead to the root cause of problems.*

Problem-Solving Truth #34: *When developing a problem statement, view the problem from two different perspectives: the object and the object's defect or fault.*

Problem-Solving Truth #35: *Symptoms are the faults we observe, so use your senses to develop the symptoms.*

Problem-Solving Truth #36: *Problems never occur without reason; they always follow changes.*

Problem-Solving Truth #37: *Identifying defect-free configurations (DFCs) is important because DFCs help us eliminate potential causes of problems.*

Problem-Solving Truth #38: *Always compare the process or object with the problem to the process or object without the problem, not vice versa. It's easier to see distinctions.*

Problem-Solving Truth #39: _Whenever possible, test to eliminate potential root causes._

Problem-Solving Truth #40: _Problems may have multiple root causes with each producing separate symptoms and each requiring separate actions._

APPENDIX B

Case Studies

THE CASE OF THE BREAKING LINKS

Problem Scenario

The Apex Motor Company has been a leader in the production of high quality DC motors since the early 1940s. Business has always been good and Apex has served a wide variety of customers. Apex has always produced small-sized motors that are used in a variety of applications. These motors typically weigh approximately 25 pounds.

Apex has always worked an A-B shift rotation, Monday through Friday. In the fall of 1992, the Apex braintrust decided it was time to expand its market and begin producing larger motors. These new motors weigh approximately 45 pounds and were to be produced at the Parker, Pennsylvania, manufacturing facility. An IE study indicated that the existing conveyor system, used to transport motors between operations, could be used if wider conveyor belts were installed. Apex completed upgrading lines 1 and 2 in early January 1993 and began production on January 19, 1993.

Sales for the new motor were much better than anyone had anticipated and Apex was having difficulty filling the orders. After much discussion, Apex decided to increase its production by extending its operations into the weekend (i.e., both Saturday and Sunday) effective January 31, 1993. Because Apex had converted two of the lines used to produce small motors, it was also having trouble filling orders for these as well. In order to meet these orders, Apex decided to extend production on lines 3 and 6 into Saturday and Sunday as well. This was also done on January 31, 1993.

On February 3, A-shift maintenance received a call that conveyor #2 had stopped running. A quick check of the conveyor revealed that the drive chain master link had broken. The link looked worn and since the conveyor was due for a PM on February 5, it was assumed that the cause of the failure was normal fatigue. The mechanic replaced the link and production resumed. On February 4, B-shift maintenance received another call that conveyor #1 had stopped. The mechanic checked out the system and found that the drive chain master link had broken. This mechanic was unaware of the problem on conveyor #2 and simply replaced the master link and production resumed again. In the next week, this problem occurred again at other times and locations as follows:

Conveyor #1	Conveyor #2	Conveyor #3	Conveyor #6
2/7: 7:00 PM	2/5: 6:13 PM	2/8: 8:20 PM	2/12: 1:00 PM
2/10: 6:15 PM	2/7: 8:22 PM	2/12: 4:32 PM	2/11: 9:11 PM

Using the PAF chart, list the most probable cause(s) and short-term and long-term solutions.

Symptoms
1. Motor conveyor stops on lines 1, 2, 3, and 6.
2. Conveyor rocks when it stops.
3. Jerky operation on lines 1 and 2.

PROBLEM ANALYSIS FLOW CHART
The Case of the Breaking Links

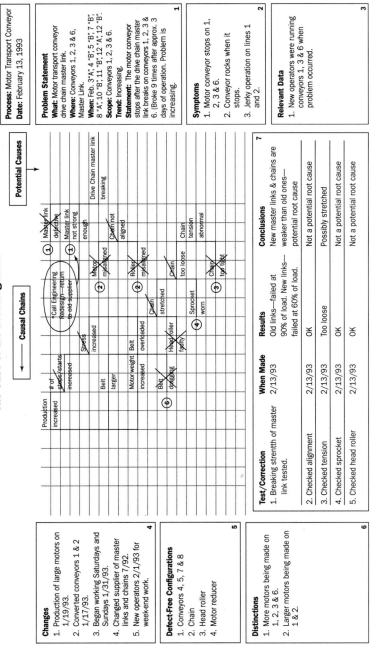

Process: Motor Transport Conveyor
Date: February 13, 1993

Problem Statement

What: Motor transport conveyor drive chain master link.
Where: Conveyors 1, 2, 3 & 6, Master Link.
When: Feb. 3 "A"; 4 "B"; 5 "B"; 7 "B"; 8 "A"; 10 "B"; 11 "B"; 12 "A"; 12 "B".
Scope: Conveyors 1, 2, 3 & 6.
Trend: Increasing.
Statement: The motor conveyor stops after the drive chain master link breaks on conveyors 1, 2, 3 & 6. (Broke 9 times after approx. 3 days of operation. Problem is increasing.

1

Symptoms

1. Motor conveyor stops on 1, 2, 3 & 6.
2. Conveyor rocks when it stops.
3. Jerky operation on lines 1 and 2.

2

Relevant Data

1. New operators were running conveyors 1, 3 & 6 when problem occurred.

3

Changes

1. Production of large motors on 1/19/93.
2. Converted conveyors 1 & 2 1/17/93.
3. Began working Saturdays and Sundays 1/31/93.
4. Changed supplier of master links and chains 7/92.
5. New operators 2/1/93 for week-end work.

4

Defect-Free Configurations

1. Conveyors 4, 5, 7 & 8
2. Chain
3. Head roller
4. Motor reducer

5

Distinctions

1. More motors being made on 1, 2, 3 & 6.
2. Larger motors being made on 1 & 2.

6

Test/Correction	When Made	Results	Conclusions
1. Breaking strentth of master link tested.	2/13/93	Old links—failed at 90% of load. New links—failed at 60% of load.	New master links & chains are weaker than old ones—potential root cause
2. Checked alignment	2/13/93	OK	Not a potential root cause
3. Checked tension	2/13/93	Too loose	Possibly stretched
4. Checked sprocket	2/13/93	OK	Not a potential root cause
5. Checked head roller	2/13/93	OK	Not a potential root cause

7

135

PROBLEM ANALYSIS FLOW CHART

Problem Statement		1	Symptoms		2	Relevant Data		3
What:								
When:								
Scope:								
Trend:								
Statement:								

Changes	4	Defect-Free Configurations	5	Distinctions	6

Test/Correction	When Made	Results	Conclusions	7
6. Checked belt drag	2/13/93	OK	Not a potential root cause	

Most Probable Cause — 9

1. New links and chains are weaker than the old ones.
2. Increased motor weight plus larger belts are stretching chains and placing added stress to master link, thus reducing their life.
3. Current master link design is not optimum (too weak).

Corrections/Controls — 10

Short Term
- Corrections
  1. Returned to supplier.
  2. Change out master links at the end of each "B" shift.
- Controls
  1. Inspect all lots of links.
  2. Maintenance check list—add link.

Long Term
- Corrections
  Redesign drive/conveyor system with stronger links/chains.
- Controls
  Establish PM after new, redesigned links/chains are implemented.

136

Relevant Data

1. New operators were running conveyors 1, 3, and 6 when problem occurred.

Changes

1. Changed supplier of master links and chains July 1992.

2. New operators began February 1, 1993, for weekend work.

3. Production of larger motors on January 19, 1993.

4. Converted conveyors 1 and 2 on January 17, 1993.

5. Began working Saturday (January 30) and Sunday January 31, 1993.

Defect-Free Configurations (DFCs)

1. Conveyors 4, 5, 7, and 8.

2. Chain

3. Head roller

4. Motor reducer

Distinctions

1. More motors being made on 1, 2, 3 & 6.

2. Larger motors being made on 1 & 2.

Tests, Corrections, Results, and Conclusions

1. Breaking strength of master link tested on February 13, 1993: New master links and chains were weaker than old ones.

2. Checked alignment on February 13, 1993: Aligned correctly.

3. Checked chain tension on February 13, 1993: Too loose, stretching chains.

4. Checked for worn sprocket on February 13, 1993: OK

5. Checked for roller alignment on February 13, 1993: OK

6. Checked for belt drag on February 13, 1993: OK

THE CASE OF THE TRIPPING OVERLOAD

Problem Scenario

The Smith Company has been producing high quality liquid filler materials since 1958. This liquid is used in a variety of applications such as waterbed gel, high viscosity lubricants with fillers, etc. Smith operates 24 hours a day and has one extended shutdown over every Christmas holiday. During this shutdown, Smith performs PMs and modifications to its equipment. The operation is highly automated with six mixing machines in operations. All of the mixing machines are PLC controlled.

In December of 1989, Smith shut down for the holidays and performed extensive modifications and PMs on all of its mixers. Upon restart, Mixer #1 began experiencing overload-tripping problems on its high-speed rotation motor. The problem was not severe, so it was essentially ignored. Mixer #1 continued to have periodic problems until May 15 when the Operations Manager stopped the operation and demanded that it be fixed once and for all. The overloads between January 2 and May 7, 1990, were as follows:

January 2	–	2:30 PM	March 17	–	1:00 AM
January 15	–	1:30 AM	March 22	–	5:17 PM
January 22	–	10:22 AM	March 28	–	6:00 AM
February 6	–	5:00 PM	April 14	–	2:33 PM
February 10	–	3:30 AM	April 19	–	4:04 AM
February 23	–	2:00 PM	April 26	–	12:01 AM
February 28	–	10:06 PM	May 7	–	1:34 PM

Using the PAF chart, determine most probable cause and short-term and long-term solutions.

PROBLEM ANALYSIS FLOW CHART
The Case of the Tripping Overload

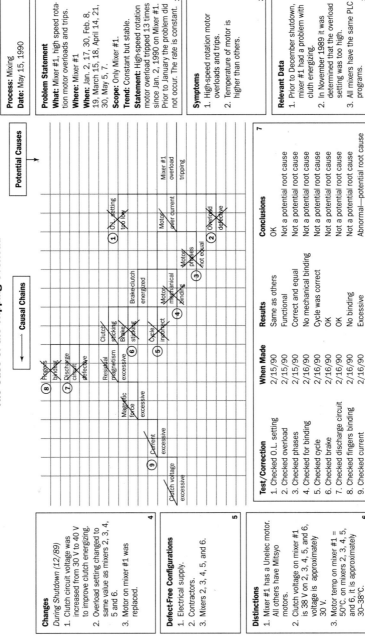

Process: Mixing
Date: May 15, 1990

← **Causal Chains** →   **Potential Causes** →

Problem Statement   1

What: Mixer #1, high speed rotation motor overloads and trips.
Where: Mixer #1
When: Jan. 2, 17, 30, Feb. 8, 19, March 15, 18, April 14, 21, 30, May 5, 7.
Scope: Only Mixer #1.
Trend: Constant but stable.
Statement: High-speed rotation motor overload tripped 13 times since Jan. 2, 1990 on Mixer #1. Prior to January the problem did not occur. The rate is constant.

Symptoms   2

1. High-speed rotation motor overloads and trips.
2. Temperature of motor is higher than others.

Relevant Data   3

1. Prior to December shutdown, mixer #1 had a problem with cluth energizing.
2. In November 1989 it was determined that the overload setting was too high.
3. All mixers have the same PLC programs.

Changes   4

During Shutdown (12/89)
1. Clutch circuit voltage was increased from 30 V to 40 V to improve clutch energizing.
2. Overload setting changed to same value as mixers 2, 3, 4, 5 and 6.
3. Motor on mixer #1 was replaced.

Defect-Free Configurations   5

1. Electrical supply.
2. Contractors.
3. Mixers 2, 3, 4, 5, and 6.

Distinctions   6

1. Mixer #1 has a Unelec motor. All others have Mitsyo motors.
2. Clutch voltage on mixer #1 is 38 V on 2, 3, 4, 5, and 6, voltage is approximately 30 V.
3. Motor temp on mixer #1 = 50°C. on mixers 2, 3, 4, 5, and 6, it is approximately 30-38°C.

Causal chain nodes: Mixer #1 overload tripping; (1) O.L. setting too low; Motor over current; (2) Overload defective; (3) Motor phases not equal; (4) Motor mechanical binding; Brake-clutch energized; (5) Cycle incorrect; (6) Brake sticking; Clutch sticking; Residual magnetism excessive; Magnetic force excessive; (7) Discharge circuit defective; (8) Fingers binding; (9) Current excessive; Clutch voltage excessive.

Test/Correction	When Made	Results	Conclusions	7
1. Checked O.L. setting	2/15/90	Same as others	OK	
2. Checked overload	2/15/90	Functional	Not a potential root cause	
3. Checked phases	2/15/90	Correct and equal	Not a potential root cause	
4. Checked for binding	2/16/90	No mechanical binding	Not a potential root cause	
5. Checked cycle	2/16/90	Cycle was correct	Not a potential root cause	
6. Checked brake	2/16/90	OK	Not a potential root cause	
7. Checked discharge circuit	2/16/90	OK	Not a potential root cause	
8. Checked fingers binding	2/16/90	No binding	Not a potential root cause	
9. Checked current	2/16/90	Excessive	Abnormal—potential root cause	

PROBLEM ANALYSIS FLOW CHART

Problem Statement 1

What:
When:
Scope:
Trend:
Statement:

Symptoms 2

Relevant Data 3

Changes 4

Defect-Free Configurations 5

Distinctions 6

Test/Correction	When Made	Results	Conclusions	7

Most Probable Cause 9

1. Clutch voltage too high, exceeds clutch rating (Distinction 2).
2. Different motor than others (Distinction 1).

Corrections/Controls 10

Short Term
- Corrections
  Reduce clutch voltage (problem stopped).
- Controls
  Establish clutch voltage.
  Check (1/shift).

Long Term
- Corrections
  Replace clutch and gearbox.
- Controls
  Establish PM-check clutch and gear box.

Symptoms
1.   High-speed rotation motor overloads and trips. 2.   Temperature of motor is higher than other motors.

Relevant Data
1. Prior to December shutdown, mixer #1 had a problem with clutch energizing. 2. In November 1989, it was determined that the overload setting was too high. 3. All mixers have the same PLC programs.

Changes
1. During shutdown clutch circuit voltage was increased from 30 V to 40 V to improve clutch energizing. 2. During shutdown overload setting changed to same values as mixers 2, 3, 4, 5, and 6. 3. Motor on mixer #1 was replaced.

Defect-Free Configurations (DFCs)
1. Electrical supply 2. Contactors 3. Mixers 2, 3, 4, 5, and 6

Distinctions
1. Mixer # 1 has a Unelec Motor, all others have Mitsuyo motor. 2. Clutch voltage on mixer #1 is 38 V; on mixers 2, 3, 4, 5, and 6, it is approximately 30 V. 3. Motor temperature on mixer #1 = 50°C; on mixers 2, 3, 4, 5, and 6, it is approximately 30–33°C.

Tests, Corrections, Results, and Conclusions			
Test/Correction	When Made	Results	Conclusions
1. Checked overload setting on mixer #1	May 15, 1990	Same as others	OK
2. Checked overload	May 15, 1990	Functional	OK
3. Checked phases	May 15, 1990	Correct and equal	OK
4. Checked for binding	May 16, 1990	No mechanical binding	OK
5. Checked cycle	May 16, 1990	Cycle was correct	OK
6. Checked brake	May 16, 1990	OK	OK
7. Checked discharge current	May 16, 1990	OK	OK
8. Checked fingers binding	May 16, 1990	No binding	OK
9. Checked residual magnetism and magnetic force	May 16, 1990	Excessive	Abnormal
10. Checked current	May 16, 1990	Excessive	Abnormal

THE CASE OF THE "BURNED UP" MOTORS

Problem Scenario

Camby Industries has been producing fiberglass parts for the automotive and trucking industry since 1958 and since then has become the recognized industry leader in terms of volume of parts produced. The current "product of choice" is Sheet Molding Compound (SMC) with parts molded in precision molds in high-pressure presses. The parts are removed from these presses and then finished on a variety of sophisticated, programmable, cutting machines. Some of these machines utilize waterjet technology while others employ the use of robotically controlled PCLs that utilize motorized routers. The PCL robots are programmed to select the correct router bits, cut the parts to specifications supplied by the customer and then return the bits to their cradle.

At the South PCL, two identical robots (Robot A and Robot B) operate simultaneously to cut or router both sides of the fiberglass part. In order to control and minimize the temperature of the motors, a chiller unit supplies coolant at predetermined temperatures. The coolant hoses are enclosed in jackets and encircle the motor to maintain the correct temperature. A coolant flow switch in the circuit is intended to divert the flow of coolant to a by-pass circuit and shut down the spindle motor when temperatures get too high to avoid damage to the motor.

On June 13, 1998, a failure in the spindle motor of Robot A was observed. A call was made to maintenance and after a brief investigation, maintenance, with no test data, concluded that the motor had burned up electrically and simply replaced the "obviously defective motor." Since very little documentation was prepared, no details were available regarding what the maintenance team had observed. No problem was observed on Robot B's motor. The defective motor was sent out to be repaired. The total downtime for this problem was 12.5 hours.

After replacement, the spindle motor seemed to work well and production resumed. After 18 hours of operation, the spindle motor stopped functioning and maintenance was called to investigate the problem. After a superficial examination of the equipment and though the chiller reservoir was found to be empty, maintenance concluded that the cause of the spindle motor failure was electrical in nature.

As before, maintenance replaced the motor and the unit was again turned over to production and the defective motor was sent out to be repaired. A total of 17 hours of downtime was incurred and, because of the frequency of failures, no "new" spindle motors were left in stock.

Robot A continued to function until July 1, 1998, when, again, the spindle motor failed. Without hesitation, maintenance simply changed the spindle motor and Robot A began functioning again. Because of the rate of failure of these motors, maintenance was forced to use a rebuilt motor that had to be air freighted into the plant at a cost of $2,000. The total amount of downtime for this occurrence was 22.75 hours.

Between July 1 and September 9, 1998, the same spindle motor failed four more times and in each case the spindle motor was replaced without a root cause analysis being conducted. Because this deviation had resulted in so much downtime and lost revenue and because so much money had been spent on motors, I was called in to assist this facility with this problem. (Remember why it is now considered a problem?) I formed a team consisting of Operations, Maintenance, and Quality/Engineering and began using a structured approach (i.e., PAF chart) to attack this problem.

The team's first step was to develop a problem statement that included answers to What, Where, When, Scope, and Trend. The following is the problem statement developed by the team.

PROBLEM STATEMENT

What: Robot A – Spindle motor

Where: South PCL – At the end of Robot A (the spindle motor)

When: June 13, 1998 @ 2:00 P.M.; June 14, 1998 @ 8:30 P.M. after 18 hours of operation; July 1, 1998 @ 6:30 P.M.; July 18, 1998 @ 4:00 P.M.; August 12, 1998 @ 2:18 A.M.; September 9, 1998 @ 3:33 P.M.; and September 11, 1998, after 20 hours of operation.

Scope: Only South PCL and only Robot A.

Trend: Increasing.

Statement: The spindle motor on Robot A stopped working at 2:00 P.M. on June 13, 1998, after no previous problems. No other spindle motors have been observed to display this problem.

Because of the lack of adequate documentation, the development of the problem statement required an extensive investigation using production downtime logs, production reports, interviews, etc.

Once the team agreed on a problem statement, they were now ready to develop a list of symptoms of the problem.

I instructed the team to observe the process using all five senses and to create a comprehensive list of symptoms. The following is the list that the team developed.

SYMPTOMS
What did we hear? Because the PCL was not running, there was nothing to hear. The team interviewed operators and concluded that there was a high-pitched sound prior to failure. The team did hear an audible alarm from the chiller reservoir.
What did we feel? Because the PCL was not running, there was nothing to feel. The team interviewed operators who explained that the housing over the motor was hot.
What did we smell? Because the PCL was not running, there was nothing to smell. The operators indicated that they had smelled the odor of burning plastic or something.
What did we see? • The rotor shaft of the spindle was locked up. • There was dark oil coming out of the gap between the rotor shaft and the front flange. • The covers were missing from all three sensor positions on the spindle. • The motor connector had arcing on the three-phase pins. • The sensor cable was cut and spliced badly. There were many splices. • The chiller reservoir was empty, the low-level chiller indicator light was lit. • The running temperature of the coolant should be no cooler than 20°C and both chillers were running at 14°C. • The sensor relays had some wires missing and some terminals jumped. • The tool changer was full of dust and the tool holder was coated with dust.

All of the above symptoms could have been related to the motor failure.

The team then developed a relevant data box as follows:

RELEVANT DATA
1. Bill Johnson was running the South PCL when the motor stopped functioning.
2. The South PCL was extremely dusty and dirty.

The team's next challenge was to investigate and develop a list of known changes along with approximate dates. This activity resulted in the following:

CHANGES
1. Changed spindle motors on June 13, June 14, July 2, July 19, August 12, September 10, and September 11, 1998.
2. Began using rebuilt motors on July 1, 1998.
3. Repaired broken sensor cables (spliced them) on June 12, 1998.
4. Replaced coolant on chiller reservoir on September 9, 1998.
5. Changed chiller unit on Robot A on May 19, 1998.

After completing the list of changes, the team then constructed a list of DFCs by comparing Robot A to Robot B and by observing the remainder of Robot A's configuration.

DEFECT-FREE CONFIGURATIONS (DFCs)
1. All of Robot B, but especially its spindle motor.
2. The remainder of Robot A's configurations except coolant flow.

Upon completion of the DFCs, the team then created a list of distinctions or differences between what is unique, special, or different between what is or is not functioning; what is unique, special, or different between where we have the problem and where we don't; or what is unique, special, or different about when we have the problem and when we don't. The distinctions were as follows:

DISTINCTIONS
1. Sensor cables were broken and spliced in Robot A, but not in Robot B.
2. The chiller reservoir was empty in Robot A, but not in Robot B.
3. The coolant tubing in Robot A was 1/4" in Robot A and 8mm in Robot B.
4. The tool proximity switches in Robot A were bypassed while not in Robot B.

Upon completion of the distinctions box, the team was ready to develop causal chains to help explain what happened to create the spindle motor problem. The following causal chains were developed.

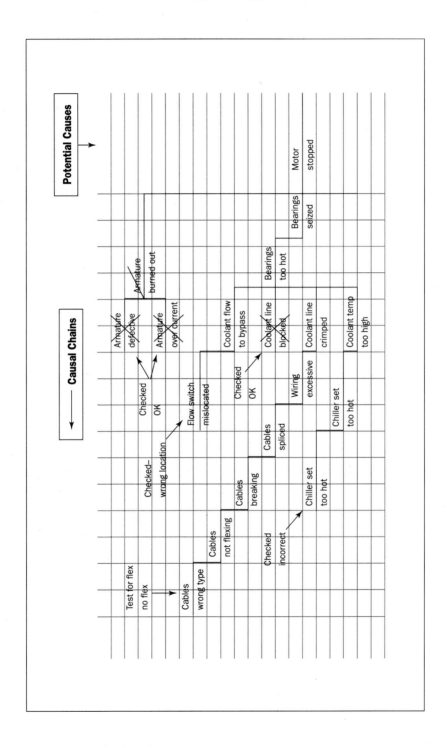

The team assumed that two possible causal chains could be responsible for the failing motors. Starting with the symptom, Motor Stopped, the team concluded that either the armature had burned out (i.e., electrical) or the bearings were seized. The team checked the armature for an over-current condition and discovered nothing was wrong with the motor electrically.

Starting with the assumption that the bearings were seized because the bearings got too hot, the team found that:

1. The coolant flow switch was mislocated and not a part of the motor cooling circuit. This was an important discovery.
2. Because of excessive wiring due to splicing of the sensor cables, the excessive wiring (i.e., splices) was actually crimping the coolant lines and restricting the flow of coolant. Because the flow switch was mislocated, it did not shut down the spindle motor, it only sent the coolant to a bypass circuit, thus allowing the motor bearings to heat to excessive temperatures and burn up.
3. Another piece to this puzzle was the temperature settings on the chiller. The temperature settings were too high.
4. The reservoir was leaking coolant so this had to be repaired.

The following are the tests and corrections made by the problem-solving team:

TESTS, CORRECTIONS, RESULTS, AND CONCLUSIONS			
Tests/Corrections	**When Made**	**Results**	**Conclusions**
Checked for over-current and/or defective armature	9/14/98	No overcurrent condition	Functionally OK
Checked for blocked coolant line	9/14/98	No blockage observed	Lines are capable of delivering coolant
Checked for location of flow switch: Corrected	9/14/98	Switch was found to be mislocated	Switch location would not shut down motor
Tested for "flexibility" of cables: Changed to more flexible cable	9/14/98	Cables were too stiff and broke easily	Cable stiffness was excessive allowing for easy breakage

Upon completion of the causal chains and the tests, corrections, results, and conclusions box, the team then discussed the most probable cause(s) and arrived at the following:

MOST PROBABLE CAUSE(S)
1. Not enough flex in the robot cables that created a breakage condition.
2. Because the robot cables broke so easily maintenance should have replaced the cables, but elected to splice them instead. This splicing created a "glut" of cables in a limited amount of space.
3. Because so many cables were spliced, there was insufficient room for the spliced cables and the flexible coolant lines thus creating a crimp in the lines and reducing or preventing the flow of coolant to the motor.
4. Because the coolant flow switch was in the wrong location, the crimping of the lines did not result in a shutdown of the spindle motor as it should have.
5. The chiller settings were found to be too high, so this was a contributing factor to the problem.

This is a classic example of multiple root causes! The team then developed appropriate corrections and controls to reduce the probability of this problem recurring.

By utilizing a structured approach to this problem, the root causes of this problem were found and appropriate corrections were made. As a result of these changes, no new occurrences of spindle motor failures have been observed.

CORRECTIONS AND CONTROLS
Short Term
Corrections
• Moved the flow switch to assure shutdown of spindle motor when coolant flow is interrupted. Updated drawing to reflect new location.
• Reset chiller settings to manufacturer's suggested settings and updated equipment documentation to reflect new settings.
• "Uncrimped" coolant lines by replacing cables when they break.
Controls
• Held training with maintenance personnel to assure everyone knew of new flow switch location, new chiller settings and why not to crimp coolant lines.
• Establish weekly audit for chiller settings and crimped coolant lines.
Long Term
Corrections
• Order and install new, flexible robot cables to reduce or eliminate cable breakage.
Controls
• Update PM Checklist to include chiller settings and functionality of flow switch.

THE CASE OF THE HIGH-PRESSURE FAULT

Problem Scenario

Since 1968, PS Industries has been producing high-quality parts for the automotive and trucking industry for over 30 years and are generally recognized as one of the leading suppliers of doors to both industries. In recent years, PS has begun using industrial adhesives instead of metal rivets to assemble its doors. All of its bonding equipment utilizes robots to apply the adhesive via pressurized dispenser units.

On July 21, 1999, PS began experiencing problems with high pressure faults on one of their bond dispense units. The problem manifested itself after periods of downtime including after breaks, lunches, maintenance interventions, quality studies, waiting for parts, etc. The production supervisor monitored the problem and discovered that after about 15 minutes of downtime, the problem with the high-pressure fault was observed. The supervisor also noted that all he had to do was reset the equipment and the bond dispense unit functioned normally. The supervisor notified maintenance and was told that they were too busy and to keep resetting the unit. The supervisor grew impatient and decided to form a team to study the problem. The supervisor selected a representative from maintenance (an electrician) and a representative from quality and engineering (a process engineer). He also selected two operators familiar with the bonding unit.

The team met and decided to use a PAF chart as their primary problem-solving tool. They began by developing their problem statement as follows:

PROBLEM STATEMENT
What: High-pressure fault on the bond dispense unit.
Where: PS 137 bonder in PS 137 bond area.
When: After periods of downtime lasting 15 minutes or longer.
Scope: Only PS 137 bonder
Trend: Constant after downtime since 7/21/99.
Statement: The PS 137 bonder stops dispensing adhesive after high-pressure fault.

The team evaluated production and downtime records, interviewed operators, and was able to develop their problem statement. By developing their problem statement, the team stayed focused on the problem.

After having completed the problem statement, the team then moved toward developing a list of symptoms. The team recalled from the problem-solving workshop training to use their five senses to develop a list of symptoms. They did so and developed the following list:

SYMPTOMS
What did we hear? The only thing the operators heard was the sound of the unit shutting down.
What did we feel? The operators explained that they did not feel anything.
What did we smell? The team did not smell any peculiar odors, just the normal smell of the adhesive.
What did we see? There were several things seen by the team as follows:
• The bonder unit stopped dispensing adhesive.
• The temperature controller was not operating properly.
• Excessive pressure build in bond dispense unit.

Having exhausted the search for symptoms, the team then began collecting other relevant data as follows:

RELEVANT DATA
1. PM was done on the bond equipment on July 20, 1999.
2. Bond dispense unit supplier suggested the use of 1/2″ bond dispense lines and 1/2″ gun tip when unit was delivered. The documentation calls for 1/4″ lines and tips.
3. Temperature was 109°F, and RH was 83.

After the team completed the relevant data box on the PAF chart, they began searching for documented changes to the process. All changes were listed as follows:

CHANGES
1. Changed adhesive supply line from 1/2″ to 1/4″ diameter as part of a July 20, 1999 PM.
2. Changed adhesive gun tip from 1/2″ to 1/4″ diameter as part of a July 20, 1999 PM.
3. New bonder operators beginning July 23, 1999.

The team knew that the root cause(s) of the problem always follows a change or changes, so it was important to take time to research to find all known changes. Because the documentation system was weak at this company, not many documented changes were found. The team was particularly interested in the two changes that occurred on July 20, 1999, since that was the day prior to the onset of the symptoms.

Having completed their change box the team now began developing the DFCs related to this equipment and created a list as follows:

DEFECT-FREE CONFIGURATIONS (DFCs)
1. All other configurations associated with the bonder in question.
2. Other bonders using the same adhesive.

Unfortunately for this team, no other bond dispense systems were identical to the one with the problem. However, because the remainder of the system was functioning normally, the team focused on that part of the system that wasn't functioning properly. One other note: other systems use the identical bond adhesive, so the team virtually ruled out any adhesive influence. Even with this limited information the team felt confident that it would solve the problem.

The team now moved to the distinctions box and listed the following:

DISTINCTIONS
1. The fault only happens when the unit is shut down for periods longer than 15 minutes. Documentation shows faults occurred after breaks, lunches, PMs, quality studies, maintenance interventions, etc.

Now that the team had completed the first six boxes on the PAF chart, it was time to create causal chains. The team took time to discuss possible root causes by using a C&E diagram. Since the team focused on just the bond dispense system (and those configurations that affected the system), it could limit the size of the causal chains. The team knew that it was looking for causes that created a back pressure high enough to cause a fault. The team, after much discussion, developed three potential causes as follows:

1. The bond dispense was being restricted creating an increase in pressure causing the fault.
2. The bond dispense unit temperature was high or low creating a high-pressure situation and then the fault.
3. The high-pressure sensor was defective thus creating a false high-pressure fault.

Using these three potential root causes, the team constructed its causal chains.

Now that the team had constructed its causal chains, they could begin analysis and elimination of potential root causes. The team constructed a list of tests to confirm or eliminate items on the causal chains as to whether or not they were root causes or not. The team also confirmed contributing factors that are indirectly responsible for the frequency or severity of the problem. Let's look at the test/correction box that the team developed:

As described earlier, the team focused on three separate causal factors:

1. A defective pressure sensor giving false indications of a problem.
2. The bond dispense unit temperature either too high or too low. Their logic was that if the viscosity of the adhesive was too high (i.e., too viscous), then a pressure buildup could occur.
3. A restriction in the adhesive delivery, thus creating a potential back-pressure problem that created the fault.

By following the causal chains and the testing the team did, we can see that the changing of the dispense line and dispense tip were probably the root causes of this problem. There were other factors that the team was not sure of, so they simply stated that potential contributing factors could not be ignored when improvements were made to the process.

CAUSAL CHAINS

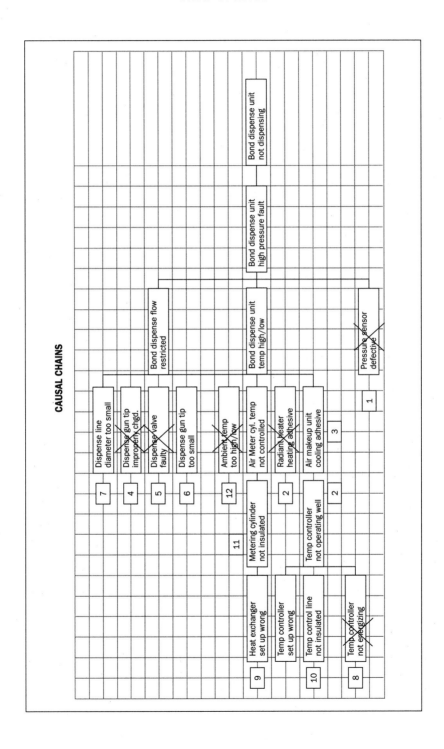

CORRECTIONS/CONTROLS
Short Term
Corrections
• Reset the equipment fault and continue to run or limit the shutdowns & startups.
Controls
• Audit to assure that operators understand the problem and are resetting the equipment.
• Issue a deviation to run by resetting until permanent fix is implemented.
Long Term
Corrections
• Change bond dispense line from 1/4″ to 1/2″ diameter.
• Change bond dispense gun tip from 1/4″ to 1/2″ diameter.
• Insulate bond temperature controller to acceptable levels.
• Insulate air metering cylinder to acceptable levels.
• Review results of problem-solving team with all maintenance mechanics.
Controls
• Update maintenance documentation and prints to reflect 1/2″ dispense line and gun tip change.
• Update PM checklist to reflect a check for line and gun tip diameters.
• Implement maintenance audit to assure completion of preventive maintenance.

Having completed testing to either eliminate or confirm those factors that were either root causes or contributing factors, the team determined, based upon the data and information collected, the root cause(s) of the problem. Let's look at the "Most Probable Cause(s)" and the recommended corrections and controls.

MOST PROBABLE CAUSE(S)
1. The dispense line was too small which caused the pressure to increase.
2. The bond gun tip was too small which caused the pressure to increase.
3. The bond temperature controller insulation was insufficient (possible contributing factor).
4. The air metering cylinder was not insulated (possible contributing factor).

The team investigated the problem, developed the most probable cause(s), developed both short-term and long-term corrective actions, and then implemented effective controls to

TESTS/CORRECTIONS/RESULTS/CONCLUSIONS

Test #	TESTS/CORRECTIONS	WHEN MADE	RESULTS/CONCLUSIONS	CONCLUSIONS
1	Checked pressure sensor for functionality	8/15/99	OK. Not defective	Functionally OK
2	Checked adhesive temperature	8/15/99	OK. Not root cause	Lines are capable of delivering coolant
3	Shut off air make-up unit	8/15/99	OK. Not root cause	
4	Observed tip changes on multiple shifts	8/15-16 99	OK. Not root cause	
5	Check adhesive ratios to determine if dispense valve is working	8/16/99	OK. Not root cause	
6	Changed gun tip from 1/2" to 1/4" diameter	8/16/99	Pressure decrease	Possible root cause
7	Changed adhesive dispense line from 1/2" to 1/4" diameter	8/16/99	Pressure decrease	Possible root cause
8	Checked temperature controller for energizing	8/16/99	OK. Not root cause	
9	Checked temperature controller heat exchanger setup	8/16/99	OK. Not root cause	
10	Checked temperature controller conditioning line insulation	8/16/99	Not enough insulation	Possible contributing factor
11	Checked air metering cylinder for insulation	8/17/99	Not insulated	Possible contributing factor
12	Checked adhesive temperature	8/17/99	Within acceptable operating range. Not root cause	Switch location would not shut down motor

157

prevent the recurrence of the problem. Once again, let's see what they did.

By using the PAF chart and the teachings in this handbook, this team was able to effectively solve this problem. The unit has run for five months without a repeat of the problem.

APPENDIX C

Sample Forms

PROBLEM ANALYSIS FLOW CHART (FRONT)

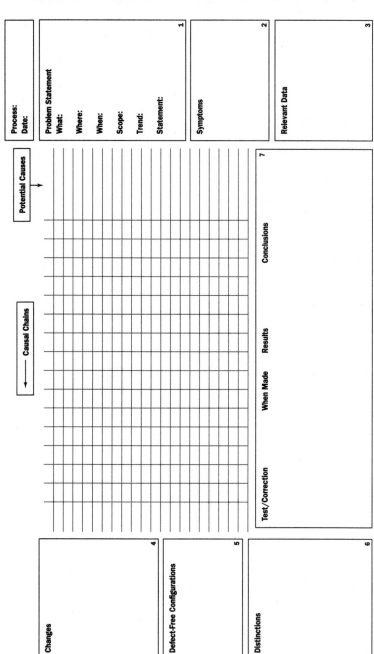

PROBLEM ANALYSIS FLOW CHART (BACK)

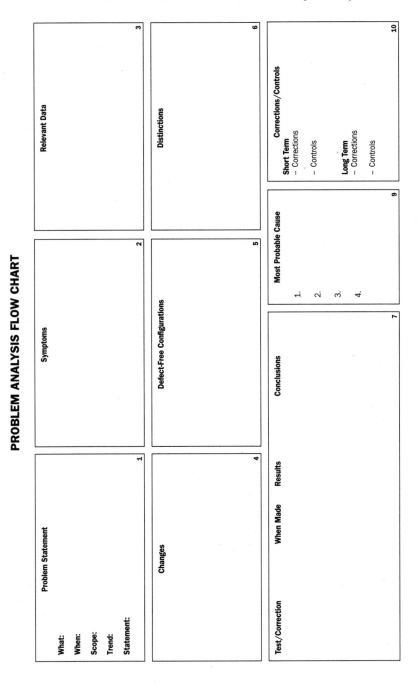

PROBLEM ANALYSIS FLOW CHART

Problem Statement 1

What:

When:

Scope:

Trend:

Statement:

Symptoms 2

Relevant Data 3

Changes 4

Defect-Free Configurations 5

Distinctions 6

Test/Correction   When Made   Results   **Conclusions** 7

Most Probable Cause 9

1.

2.

3.

4.

Corrections/Controls 10

Short Term
– Corrections

– Controls

Long Term
– Corrections

– Controls

CAUSE & EFFECT DIAGRAM

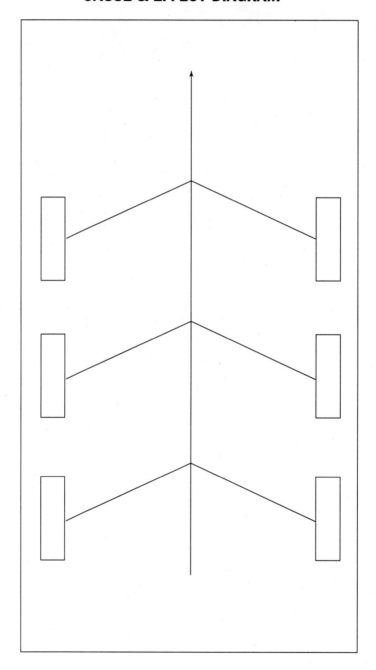

CAUSE & EFFECT DIAGRAM

SCATTERGRAM OR RUN CHART

SCATTERGRAM OR RUN CHART

Y	
X	

References

1. Kepner and Tregoe, *The New Rational Manager* (Kepner-Tregoe, Incorporated, 1981).

2. Ishikawa, Kaoru, *Guide to Quality Control* (Asia Productivity Organization, 1986).

3. Bailie, Howard H., "Organize Your Thinking With a Why?-Why? Diagram." *Quality Progress*, December 1985.

Index

Productivity, Inc. Consulting, Training, Workshops, and Conferences

EDUCATION...IMPLEMENTATION...RESULTS

Productivity, Inc. is the leading American consulting, training, and publishing company focusing on delivering improvement technology to the global manufacturing industry.

Productivity prides itself on delivering today's leading performance improvement tools and methodologies to enhance rapid, ongoing, measurable results. Whether you need assistance with long-term planning or focused, results-driven training, Productivity's world-class consultants can enhance your pursuit of competitive advantage. In concert with your management team, Productivity will focus on implementing the principles of Value-Adding Management, Total Quality Management, Just-in-Time, and Total Productive Maintenance. Each approach is supported by Productivity's wide array of team-based tools: Standardization, One-Piece Flow, Hoshin Planning, Quick Changeover, Mistake-Proofing, Kanban, Problem Solving with CEDAC, Visual Workplace, Visual Office, Autonomous Maintenance, Overall Equipment Effectiveness, Design of Experiments, Quality Function Deployment, Ergonomics, and more! And, based on continuing research, Productivity expands its offering every year.

Productivity's conferences provide an excellent opportunity to interact with the best of the best. Each year our national conferences bring together the leading practitioners of world-class, high-performance strategies. Our workshops, forums, plant tours, and master series are scheduled throughout the U.S. to provide the opportunity for continuous improvement in key areas of lean management and production.

Productivity, Inc. is known for significant improvement on the shop floor and the bottom line. Through years of repeat business, an expanding and loyal client base continues to recommend Productivity to their colleagues. Contact us at 1-800-394-6868 to learn how we can tailor our services to fit your needs.